Leadership and Management in the Early Years

A practical guide to building confident leadership skills

by Jane Cook

Contents

Published by Practical Pre-School Books, A Division of MA Education Ltd,
St Jude's Church, Dulwich Road, Herne Hill, London, SE24 0PB.

Tel: 020 7738 5454

www.practicalpreschoolbooks.com

© MA Education Ltd 2013.

Photos taken by Lucie Carlier. All photos © MA Education Ltd.

ISBN 978-1-907241-42-0

Early
Childhood
Essentials

Effective leadership makes a difference

"Leadership and learning are indispensable to each other" John F. Kennedy.

This book has been written for everyone with a leadership role, or thinking about a leadership role, within the early years sector. It has been inspired by all the creative, passionate, clever, hard-working, funny and determined leaders I have worked with during the past thirty years.

Working in the early years, we know that good quality education and care makes a difference to children's lives and that this continues to have positive impact many years after the child has left the setting. The role of the leader in creating the quality to make that difference, is crucial. All the research is telling us that the quality of provision and children's outcomes almost never exceeds the quality of leadership and management.

"….there is no doubt that effective leadership and appropriate training for the leadership role is an increasingly important element in providing high quality provision for the early years" Siraj-Blatchford and Manni (2007).

Why leadership in the early years matters

"We must be the change we wish to see in the world" Mahatma Gandhi.

Those of us working in early years have always known how important our work is. We know that a child is only a baby, a toddler, a young child once – and it's vital that we make that experience the very best possible for every child. We also know that early childhood is the foundation upon which all future development depends. We are rightly proud when our young children move to a primary school confident and excited about their own abilities and feeling secure about their place in the world.

The greater the change and uncertainty, the more important it is to hold on to your core values about early childhood education. These are expressed in the EYFS as:

Theme: A Unique Child

Principle: Every child is a competent learner from birth who can be resilient, capable, confident and self-assured.

Theme: Positive Relationships

Every child is a competent learner from birth, who can be resilient, capable, confident and self-assured

Principle: Children learn to be strong and independent from a base of loving and secure relationships with parents and/or a key person.

Theme: Enabling Environments

Principle: The environment plays a key role in supporting and extending children's development and learning.

Theme: Learning and Development

Principle: Children develop and learn in different ways and at different rates and all areas of Learning and Development are equally important and interconnected.

As a leader in the early years you make a difference for children and their families

Lasting impact

Since the beginning of the 21st Century there has been steadily increasing interest from outside the sector in what can be achieved through high quality early years education and care. For example, in the UK this has led to the introduction of free nursery education (initially for all three- and four-year-olds and most recently 40% of two-year-olds), Children's Centres (and the links this has helped to make with professionals in health and social care), the Early Years Professional Status, Graduate Leader Fund, Early Years Foundation Stage and a review of qualifications for the early years workforce.

Graham Allen, in his report on Early Intervention in 2011, put early years at the heart of his proposals to change the life chances of those most at risk of underachievement. The photograph on the front cover of the report shows the brains of two three-year-old children. The first brain is of a child who has had the support and love needed to thrive, and the second of a child who has already suffered from extreme neglect. The size of the second child's brain is significantly smaller than that of first child. The photograph was designed to shock, and it worked.

"*The rationale is simple: many of the costly and damaging social problems in society are created because we are not giving children the right type of support in their earliest years, when they should achieve their most rapid development*" Graham Allen Report on Early Intervention 2011.

What happens in the early years is not only of vital importance for the well-being of our youngest children, it also has a profound and lasting impact on their ability to have a happy and fulfilling life. Your role as a leader in early years – working with your team, with parents and with other professionals to create the best possible provision for the children in your care, is therefore one of the most important jobs there is.

In this book we will look at the knowledge, skills and attributes you have as an early years practitioner and consider how you can develop them further to maximise your confidence, skills and impact as a leader. The ideas and concepts are all firmly rooted in research, but the approach is always practical.

We begin by looking at some different approaches to understanding leadership and leaders and the implications for leading in the early years sector.

Later chapters go into more detail about the knowing, doing and being of different aspects of leadership, including the importance of effective supervision.

Chapter 1

Introducing the early years leader

Effective leadership practice

"*Today a reader, tomorrow a leader*"
Margaret Fuller, 19th Century Women's Rights Activist.

This is an exciting time to be working in early years, but it is also a challenging one for leaders and practitioners across the sector. With more attention, comes increased expectation and accountability. With more opportunity, comes increased complexity and demands on time. In an implicit acknowledgement of the range and scope of the leadership role in the early years, Iram Siraj-Blatchford and Laura Manni

Observing children will have strengthened our empathy and reflective skills

identified ten categories of 'effective leadership practice' (Institute of Education, 2007) as follows:

1. **Identifying and articulating a collective vision**

2. **Ensuring shared understanding, meanings and goals**

3. **Effective communication**

4. **Encouraging reflection**

5. **Monitoring and assessing practice**

6. **Commitment to ongoing, professional development**

7. **Distributed leadership**

8. **Building a learning community and team culture**

9. **Encouraging and facilitating parent and community partnerships**

10. **Leading and managing: striking the balance.**

This may look a daunting list, but the experience of an early years practitioner provides an excellent foundation for leadership. When practitioners move from working with children to leading adults, what is most often emphasised is the difference between the two roles. There are differences, which mean there will be areas for learning and development to explore throughout this book. But there are also huge similarities. From working with children and their families we will have developed a huge range of useful communication skills. In planning an environment we will have built up organisational and planning skills. Observing children will have strengthened our empathy and reflective skills. Above all, we will have carried with us a vision for quality that will continue to develop and inspire us throughout our professional lives.

In brief, as leaders, we do not start from scratch if we have been effective early years practitioners. We may have a lot to learn about leadership (and how boring would our work be if we didn't have things still to learn!) but we have a lot to bring to the role too.

Communication

"I listen to children all the time. I know how important it is for our relationship, as well as developing speech and language. I suddenly realised I never listened to my staff. I always thought I was too busy, that listening to adults wasn't part of my job. I now realise what a lot I was missing. It doesn't take long either. You can learn a lot in five minutes proper listening" (Lucy, a pre-school head).

What skills, knowledge and attributes have you developed as a practitioner in:

- Improving quality?

- Communicating meaningfully with children and adults?

- Working in a team?

- Supporting learning and development for children and adults?

What are the implications for you in your role as a leader?

What other skills or attributes have you developed as a practitioner that you can see supporting you in your role as a leader?

Leadership styles

Many people used to think that leaders were 'born' so, that they were either 'natural leaders' or they weren't. Nowadays, most people agree that anybody can learn how to lead given the right kind of opportunity, support and challenge. Increasingly research is also telling us that there isn't one 'perfect' leadership style, but many. The key to success as a leader lies in making sure that we have a style that draws on our natural strengths, and learning how to develop that to include other skills, attributes and knowledge to help us meet our leadership challenges with confidence and flexibility.

How do we find out what our natural style or approach might be? For many of us in our first leadership positions, the

We need to remember to find time to listen to practitioners, as well as children

most influential person on our style will be a leader we have experienced ourselves. If the experience of being 'led' by that person was a good one, we will tend to follow their example. If it was a negative experience we are likely to try and adopt a style that is the opposite of what we observed.

Influences

"When I became head of centre I know I modelled my leadership style on Liz, who'd been my favourite manager. She used to make us all feel so valued we'd do anything for her. She had lots of good ideas herself, but she was also really good at letting us come up with ideas and then just go with them. It was always interesting working there. She didn't forget the little things either, like cakes after a difficult week or asking after my daughter who'd been in hospital" (Alice, a practitioner).

"I liked my last boss a lot. She was kind and friendly and was passionate about the children, but she was really difficult to work for. She was always changing her mind about things so you were never sure where you were.

You'd just get used to one routine and there'd be another one! Or we'd start to work on developing the book area but then move onto the outdoor space before we'd finished. I was exhausted and confused! I don't want my staff to feel like that so I'm really careful to work out a plan together and then stick to it" (Charmaine, a practitioner).

Think about people who have influenced your leadership style:

What did they do, say and think that was important?

What is useful in their style for you to take away – and why?

What might be less useful? Why?

We can learn much from our mentors, but it is also useful to look more widely at different approaches to leadership. Daniel Goleman, in his book *The New Leaders*, argues that the best leaders are those that use a range of different styles depending on both their personal preferences and the needs of any particular situation. He identified six styles that he argues are the ones most used by effective leaders. Two of them have to be used very carefully to avoid a potentially negative impact on the team. Goleman suggests that to be an effective leader you need to be comfortable in using flexibly at least four out of the six according to circumstances. If you read through the list you will probably find that you are more drawn to some styles than others. Many times you will be drawing on more than one style at a time to meet the needs of the moment.

The visionary leader uses a positive, forward moving style

LINKS WITH YOUR PRACTICE

Read about the leadership styles identified by Daniel Goleman et al. in the table on page 7. Think about where you have experienced examples of the different styles in practice. How effective were they?

POINT FOR REFLECTION

"Great leaders, the research shows, are made as they gradually acquire, in the course of their lives and careers, the competences that make them so effective. The competences can be learned by any leader, at any point" Goleman, D (2002).

Characteristics, skills and roles

Just as when we are working with children we know how important it is to look at the 'whole child', likewise it can be very useful to look at the leader in a holistic way too. Who we are and what we know and understand can influence our leadership style as much as our skills.

Jillian Rodd, in *Leadership in Early Childhood*, looks at leadership through a lens of personal characteristics, professional skills and roles and responsibilities. This can be helpful in starting to identify where our strengths lie, and what might be particular areas for development. Her personal characteristics include kind, warm, friendly, nurturing, sympathetic and rational, logical and analytical. Few of us will naturally feel that all these words describe us. We may find it easier to empathise with staff than to be logical and analytical with them about their areas for development. We may feel very comfortable with using logic and analysis to make decisions, but feel more uncomfortable checking with parents what the impact of that decision might be on their values and priorities. Read about the leadership styles identified by Daniel Goleman et al. in the table on page 7. Think about where your strengths might lie.

Leadership Styles: Based on the Leadership Repertoire in 'The New Leaders' (2002) Goleman, D., Boyatzis, R. and McKee, A.

Leadership Style	Main features	Example
Visionary	The visionary leader moves people towards shared dreams using a positive, forward moving style. This style is most useful when clear direction is required or a new vision is needed following a change in circumstances. It can be poorly used when the leader is working with a team that is much more experienced and knowledgeable than she is and feel they don't need a "new vision". Another danger is for the leader to get too caught up in her own "vision" and not realise everyone is not on board with her.	Sharon has taken over the management of a pre-school after a very poor Ofsted. She needs to persuade the demoralised staff team that there is a better future for the pre-school and that they can get there together and so a visionary style is perfect for her. It helps to recreate a sense of purpose for the team and trust in the organisation's capacity for improvement.
Coaching	The coaching leader also has a positive style, using empathy to build trust and a balance of support and challenge to move practice forward. This style is particularly effective at building up highly skilled and experienced teams of motivated staff. Used well, the coaching style allows the leader to give positive and negative feedback constructively. When used poorly, a leader can drift into micro-management or over-control.	Sharon knows that the practitioners have very low confidence in their knowledge and skills following the poor Ofsted. She uses a coaching approach to help move practice forward. She reinforces the positive at every opportunity and uses a sensitive mixture of support and challenge to create the energy and resourcefulness for change.
Affiliative	The affiliative leader is particularly skilled at bringing harmony to a team, helping to motivate staff during difficult times, heal tensions and discord and strengthen positive working connections. When used on its own, the affiliative style can drift into a directionless quagmire where poor performance is ignored and work always takes second place to relationships.	Sharon recognised that before her coaching could have real impact she needed to build morale and trust. She spent a lot of time with each member of the team, listening to their views and taking them into account as she adapted the timetable and routines of the pre-school. She brought in small treats for the staff and was generous with praise to rebuild morale. Because she was also using a visionary approach, she was able to simultaneously focus on high standards and improving quality.
Democratic	The democratic leader values people's input and uses this to build a strong consensus of agreement for the work of the setting. The practitioners feel "ownership" of the plans and policies and are therefore more likely to commit to doing their best at work? The democratic approach does not work when the practitioners do not have the knowledge to make an informed choice or where an urgent decision is required.	Andrew is the chair of the pre-school management committee and he is keen to achieve 'buy-in' to all the necessary changes from the staff team. He is a very experienced chair and is clear about where a democratic approach can work and where it would be unhelpful. Working with Sharon he finds it helpful to get the staff view on a new logo for the pre-school and plans to expand the outdoor area. Other discussions about the lease and staff contracts are kept confidential.
Pacesetting	The pacesetting leader is full of energy and drive. She is focused on meeting challenging and exciting goals. At her best she gets very fast, high quality results from a motivated and competent team. If used poorly or excessively, the pacesetting approach can leave practitioners feeling confused, inadequate and demoralised. Since pacesetters often focus on goals without appearing to care for the people, the result can be high levels of anxiety and mistrust – which are a disaster for making progress. The irony is that by focusing too much on increasing the pace of change, the result can be to go backwards.	Despite the pressure on them to get results quickly, neither Sharon nor Andrew adapt a pacesetting approach with their team as they recognise that this would just push team confidence and morale lower still and slow progress further. In another pre-school, Zenab, is using the pacesetting approach brilliantly. They've been waiting for a refurbishment for eighteen months. Staff morale was low because they'd felt completely "stuck". Once the building work was completed, Zenab and her highly competent team could throw themselves 100% into their long awaited plans, responding with energy and enthusiasm to Zenab's pace-setting approach.

Leadership Styles: Based on the Leadership Repertoire in 'The New Leaders' (2002)
Goleman, D., Boyatzis, R. and McKee, A. continued

Leadership Style	Main features	Example
Commanding	This is another approach that needs to be used cautiously. The typical commander gives orders and expects them to be followed without question. Some of our most famous war leaders will have used a commanding style. It can be very helpful in a crisis, reassuring people that everything is going to work out fine. It is can also be useful when people need to be "shocked" into realising that things have to change or as a last resort with members of staff with competency or compliance issues. However, generally in the early years sector this is not a style that is going to engage and motivate staff.	Luckily for Sharon she didn't need to "shock" her team into realising they needed to do things differently – they were ready and willing to start to improve from day one. In a local maintained school the situation was different. Ofsted had given the whole school a "good" but only rated the foundation stage as "satisfactory" – at best. The foundation stage leader reacted by saying that Ofsted had got it wrong and they didn't need to change anything. After several weeks of trying a coaching and affiliative approach, the headteacher had to use a "commanding" style to bring home the message that "no change" was not an option. The Foundation Stage Coordinator (FSCO) could either start to work with the Deputy (who was also experienced in early years) on an action plan or face disciplinary measures.

Jillian Rodd: Typology of a leader

Personal characteristics	Professional skills	Roles and responsibilities
Kind, warm, friendly	Technical competence as an early childhood professional to act as a model, guide and mentor	To deliver and be accountable for a quality service
Nurturing, sympathetic		To develop and articulate a philosophy, values and vision
Patient		
Self-aware	General administration	To engage in a collaborative and partnership approach to learning
Knowledgeable		To engage in ongoing professional development and to encourage it in all staff
Rational, logical, analytical	Financial management	
Professional, professionally confident	Effective communication	To be sensitive and responsive to the need for change and manage change effectively
Visionary		
Mentor and guide, empowering	Human resource management	
Assertive, proactive		
Goal orientated		To act as an advocate for children, parents, staff, the profession and general community

KEY POINTS IN INTRODUCING THE EARLY YEARS LEADER

In this chapter you have been introduced to some different ways of looking at leadership skills, tasks, attributes, knowledge. Use the lists from Siraj-Blatchford and Manni, Goleman and Rodd to help you think about your own approach to leadership.

○ Where do you think your strengths might lie?

What do you enjoy doing most?

What aspects of leadership to you least enjoy?

What are the areas of leadership or the approaches that you feel least confident with?

Chapter 2

The reflective leader

*"Becoming a leader is synonymous with becoming yourself.
It is precisely that simple, and it is also that difficult"*
Warren G. Bennis, Leadership Guru (b.1925).

The most important resource you have in your role as a leader, is always going to be yourself: your skills, your knowledge, your experience and your personal attributes. By knowing more accurately what kind of a leader you are now, you will be better able to identify what steps you need to take to become the leader you want to be. That knowledge comes from two main sources: the quality of feedback you get on your performance as a leader, and your ability to self-reflect and analyse what you do, why you do it and what the impact is on you, your setting and your community.

In a lively setting with many competing demands from staff, parents, children and administration, it's not always easy to find the time to think and reflect.

Reflective journal

One way of building thinking time into a busy working day is by starting a reflective journal. Buy yourself a notebook that you are going to enjoy writing in and for collecting thoughts and bits of information. Some people have compared their journals to the portfolios and learning journeys we create for children. You can record your thoughts, ask yourself questions, note interesting pieces of information and doodle. You can also stick in interesting articles and notes – for example a letter from a parent thanking you for something special.

A useful place to start is by jotting down what's been really important to you in your career to date. Think about the high points; what made you feel happy or proud? Think about the points where you felt demotivated or anxious. What was happening then? You may also want to include some reference to other important life events outside the sphere of work but

which have had a significant impact on your life – for example, having children or doing a language course.

You may find it useful to complete a 'lifeline' like the one on the next page to template below to start your thinking. Your reflective journal will always be private to you so you should feel completely free to record what is important to you.

Using her lifeline (p.10) to reflect on her career to date, Caro noted in her journal that she realised that the ethos of the place she worked was really important to her, that she needed to feel valued and supported to do her best and that criticism left her feeling unconfident and anxious – not able to do her job properly.

Using a journal can help you reflect about your leadership role

Caro's example lifeline

Date	Event	High	Medium	Low
1993	Work experience at Brightside Day Nursery – loved it and got great feedback.	x		
1995	Left school – school was OK (esp NVQ), but really was looking forward to leaving and getting to work.		x	
1996	First Job – St. Andrew's pre-school. Great team, very supportive – learned lots from them and had opportunity to go on courses too.	x		
2001	New manager – didn't get on with the team, everything felt negative, always being criticised. On the plus side it motivated me to apply for my foundation degree and then get promotion to my next setting. So it's probably a medium.		x	
2003	Honeyside Children's Centre – 0-3 coordinator – fantastic job, lots going on, very creative and positive atmosphere. Had baby and started job-share. Enjoyed that – found I like working with adults as well as with children!	x		
2009	Moved to Debdale Children's Centre as Deputy. Felt very proud at first – I'd been asked to apply by the local authority who had liked my work at Honeyside. Struggled a bit to begin with as I was working full time again (and that was difficult to juggle with my own childcare). I lost confidence for a while as the head of centre was too busy to really spend much time with me.			x
2010	Still finding the new job a challenge, but having a mentor in another children's centre is really helping. She's helping me feel more confident about what I have to offer and also to be better at being clear about what I need for my own development. I'm also learning more about how to ask Su (my manager) for support – when I'm clear about what I need she's always there for me, I just have to remember to ask! I'm even thinking of applying to do my NPQICL with her encouragement. I'm putting my work as a medium at the moment as I know I've still got a lot of work to do on my own self-confidence and that makes this job hard – but I know I'll get there in the end!		x	

So being positive and motivating with adults as well as children was something she would look to do herself as a leader. The other thing that struck her was that her school experience had left her feeling very unconfident with authority figures, like her new head of centre, but that she was now learning how to be more assertive and confident – and it felt good!

Your own reflection

Looking at your own lifeline – what strikes you most about your career to date? What were the high points? Do you know why? What were the low points? What was happening for you to describe it as low? Who else was involved? What were they doing? Are there any patterns that you notice?

Now sit back and reflect. What has been really important to you that you can use in your leadership development? Is there anything that you need to let go of – a worry or anxiety that is holding you back? For Caro, one of her learning points was the realisation that she was worried about being assertive sometimes, especially with authority figures.

Caro had a mentor that she could talk to. Do you have a mentor, either formal or informal? If not, who do you go to for your most important professional discussions? Use your reflective journal to list the names of people in your professional network. They could be other leaders and managers you have worked with in the past, colleagues in other settings or someone from school you've kept in touch with. If you are finding it difficult to choose the right person, your local authority or regional office might be able to suggest someone.

Balance wheel

The 'lifeline' exercise helps us to put into context our career up to this point, the positive and not so positive experiences and the influence they may have had on our development as a leader. Another useful exercise to include at the beginning of your reflective journal is the 'Balance wheel' (see diagram 13 for an example).

As practitioners we are all very aware of how important it is to care for the 'whole child' and not just focus on bits of the curriculum or areas of development at the expense of others. The same thing is true for us as adults. Having looked at where you've come from, the Balance wheel gives you the opportunity to step back from your work as it is now and look at the complete picture. It is a very useful exercise that can give you all kinds of insights into what your priorities are now and how you are thinking and feeling about them individually and as a group.

What different things do you do in your role as a leader?

You need to start by thinking of all the things that you do in your role as a leader and listing them on a piece of paper. Some of the things that have arisen when working with leaders in different settings have included:

- Meetings with parents
- Working with the children
- Observing children
- Assessing children
- Monitoring the progress of children
- Working on the environment
- Liaising with other professionals
- Continuing professional development
- Private study
- Action planning

- Completing administrative forms
- Managing the premises
- Organising rotas and timetables
- Staff supervision and performance management
- Governance – reporting to advisory boards or trustees
- Working on the budget
- Marketing
- Ordering or managing resources
- Health and safety
- Safeguarding
- Staff meetings
- Staff development

- Communication, eg emails and phone calls, newsletters

- Development of policies and procedures.

From your list, try and identify 7-10 key areas of work that you do most weeks. You may decide to group some of the tasks together in a way that makes sense to how you work in your setting (e.g. working on the budget and managing resources might be one area). Put each one in an area of the blank balance wheel.

Glenda's Wheel

Glenda grouped her work into 8 areas. She marked her levels of satisfaction (1-10, 1 being low) as:

Children 7 – *because I enjoy that part of my work the most, but I don't feel I have time to do it so much anymore and I worry that's stopping me being so effective in supporting the staff in their work.*

Staff 5 – *they're a great team and always very supportive but I don't feel confident in helping them to develop their practice*

What is the most important part of your job?

Parents 9 – *I think this is a strength in our setting. We're all really good at finding time to talk with the parents and they're great at coming in and sharing things with us – like Albanian nursery rhymes and the display for Hanukkah.*

Finances 8 – *this surprised me because I thought it was my worst area, but actually we've have great support on this and I'm finding it quite straightforward.*

Curriculum 6 – *this surprised me too as learning and development had always been my strength but I think I've taken my eye of the ball for a while and things have started to drift. I've not had time to monitor the planning and it's all getting a bit "samey".*

Administration 8 – *it takes up far too much of my time, but actually I think I'm pretty much on top of it.*

Development 4 – *I can see I've been focusing on the everyday stuff and not really thought about where we might be going to next. I know the local authority is keen to support us doing 'forest school', this might be the time to ask them what that would involve.*

Emails 2 – *I counted the time I spent on this yesterday and couldn't believe it. I've got to find a better way of managing this.*

All in all I think I'm having a very bumpy ride at the moment. I seem to be spending most of my time on the areas I don't think are that important and letting some of the really big things slip. I'm actually quite shocked at the scores I've given myself for areas that I think of as my strengths. Perhaps as a new manager I was focusing too much on the areas that were new and that I didn't feel so confident about. Next week I'm going to start spending more time in the rooms with the staff and children and get some sparkle back into that planning!

Choosing your own headings, draw yourself a wheel made out into segments like Glenda's. With 0 at the centre and 10 on the edge, decide how satisfied you are with each area of your work on the balance wheel. Then draw a line across the segment to show your level of satisfaction (see diagram on page 13 for an example).

Ask yourself these questions to help you decide what score to give for each area:

- Do you enjoy this area of work?

- How important is this area of work to you?

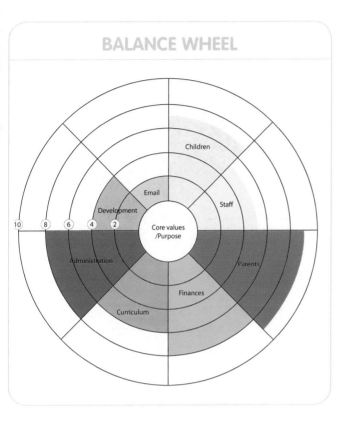

BALANCE WHEEL

(Children, Email, Staff, Development, Core values /Purpose, Administration, Parents, Finances, Curriculum)

10 8 6 4 2

The four Johari Windows are called 'areas' and each contains a different set of information about the person depending on whether it is known by the person themselves, or by others, by both or by neither as follows:

- **Open area** – what is known by the person about him/herself and is also known by others

- **Blind area** – what is unknown by the person him/herself but of which others are aware

- **Hidden area** – what the person knows about him/herself that others do not know

- **Unknown area** – what is unknown by the person him/herself and also unknown by others.

According to the theory, our aim should be to make the open area as big as possible because it is when we are working in this area we are all at our most effective. Leaders that know themselves well, their strengths and their weaknesses, and who are able to share these openly with their team, build up an ethos of trust and respect. If we do not know what our teams are finding difficult about us it can lead to misunderstandings and distrust.

- How much of your time does it take? Is that enough?

- How pleased are you with the quality of your work in this area?

- What else might you like to do?

- What feedback have you had from others on this area of work?

When you have finished, look at your wheel. How bumpy would your ride be? What strikes you about your work overall, and for the different areas? What might you want to look at differently for the future to create a more 'balanced' wheel?

We need to be thoughtful too about what we decide to keep hidden about ourselves. How much we feel comfortable about disclosing will vary depending on our different personalities and circumstances. It is important for a manager to keep some things confidential, for example, issues with individual members of staff. Some things it is wiser to keep close, for example, a manager who loudly and regularly complains about their responsibilities and concerns in the setting can cause anxiety and stress amongst the team.

The Johari window

"*What is necessary to change a person is to change his awareness of himself*" Abraham H. Maslow.

'The Johari window' was developed by management consultants Luft and Ingham and is named after combing their first names. By providing us with insight into how others might perceive us and how we share information about ourselves with others, it helps us to understand more about our feelings, attitudes, skills and motivation. The model introduces four different perspectives.

The Johari window

Unknown by others	Hidden area	Unknown area
Unknown by others	Open area	Blind area
	Known by self	Unknown by self

The benefits of feedback

Mina, a new foundation stage coordinator in a busy primary school. The previous coordinator was conscientious, but the curriculum planning and environment had been getting a little tired.

In Mina's Open area are her enthusiasm, her energy and her passion for making a difference for the children. This has helped her build up some positive relationships within the team who see her commitment and respect her knowledge and expertise. In Mina's Blind area is her tendency to talk over people in meetings as she gets carried away with her enthusiasm. Some of the team are beginning to see this as a lack of respect for their views – and they are starting to dig in their heels against some of the changes. She also talks very fast about things that she understands but can leave others behind, feeling nervous and unconfident about their ability to take forward the proposed changes. In Mina's Hidden area is her worry that if the school had an inspection at the moment they would have a very poor result. She's not very confident about giving negative feedback and had hoped to move quickly with the developments without having to upset anyone by appearing to be critical about

what had been there before. In Mina's Unknown area is her unconscious assumption that being honest about her concerns will turn everyone against her.

The result for Mina was that the she and the staff were starting to drift further and further apart. They misunderstood her communication style and didn't tell her and so she thought that they were just ganging up against her and resistant to any change. What rescued the situation was feedback. The headteacher had observed a staff meeting and fed back to Mina what she had seen – that the staff did not understand her plans and that Mina wasn't giving them enough time to contribute to the discussions. Together, Mina and the headteacher planned the next staff meeting to ensure that everybody was involved and had time to think and reflect about Mina's suggestions – and make some of their own. The headteacher also encouraged Mina to be honest with the team about where she saw the quality of the setting at the moment – giving praise to what was going well, but explaining why they needed to make some changes to better meet the requirements of the EYFS.

LINKS WITH YOUR PRACTICE

Your professional network

Many years ago, when I had my first leadership position, someone gave me a metaphor about how to manage with new or challenging situations. She called it the 'Swamp Theory' and explained it like this: imagine you are a frog at the edge of a huge swamp. It's full of dangers so you can't swim across. Across the surface is a path of lily pads and so you use those to get from one side to the other without falling into the swamp. When your work is feeling particularly challenging, think of it as being like the swamp, and imagine that your professional network is like the lily pads – with their help you can get to the other side safe and sound.

Write a list in your journal of all the people you have in your professional network.

- Who would you phone if you were having a crisis and needed authoritative advice?

- Who would you trust to give you honest feedback on your own performance as a leader?

- Who is a good listener?

Who would you phone for advice and help?

POINT FOR REFLECTION

Later in the book we will look in more detail at how leaders can give effective feedback to their teams to build confidence and motivation, whilst also addressing areas that need development. For this chapter, the important point is to start making sure that you get honest feedback for yourself so that you can build up a stronger ethos of trust, openness and cooperation, avoiding confusion, misunderstandings and unnecessary conflict. Mina was lucky in having a headteacher she trusted and respected. Think about who you trust and respect that you could ask for feedback from. It may be a colleague you've known for some years and works in another setting, or a manager you've worked for previously and kept in touch with. It could be your deputy or someone on your board of trustees.

Developing a feedback culture

Your professional network and your mentors are excellent sources of feedback, but you can get equally useful feedback from your team. Building a culture where you as the leader are regularly asking for feedback and are seen to be reflecting on what people say and, where appropriate, changing your behaviour, helps to create a learning culture for the whole setting. If your team see you as open to feedback as part of your everyday practice, they are more likely to be open to feedback themselves. For example…

After a performance management meeting: Can I ask you for some feedback? How useful was this session for you? Which part did you find most helpful? Was there anything I could have done differently that could have made it more constructive?

After a staff meeting: Can I ask you for some feedback? We talked about some important issues today; did everybody feel they had a chance to have their say? Does anybody need more information on anything? Did we cover everything important?

After a carpet session: That was an interesting session – I was trying something I hadn't done before. Can I ask you for some feedback? Do you think all the children were joining in? Which bit of the activity do you think they enjoyed most? If I did it again, what do you think I should do differently?

Don't be surprised if when you first start asking for feedback you get: "It was fine" – it can take a while for people to realise you really want to know, not just get some praise. It helps to have specific questions as in some of the examples above.

Later in the book we will look in more detail at how leaders can give effective feedback to their teams to build confidence and motivation, whilst also addressing areas that need development. For this chapter, the important point is to start making sure that you get honest feedback for yourself so that you can build up a stronger ethos of trust, openness and cooperation, avoiding confusion, misunderstandings and unnecessary conflict.

One way of talking about our ability to self-reflect and analyse our strengths and weaknesses is called Emotional

The emotional life of a nursery

Time	Facts	Emotions
7.00am	Phone call from member of staff to say she's sick and won't be coming in.	**Irritation** – it's the third time this month and you should have been going on a course, which now looks unlikely. But you know she's been struggling in for the last few days so you are calm and professional – but then rush off to work to see if you can sort out the rota.
8.30am	You realise that you can't go on the course – no cover is available.	You're **disappointed** about the course and a bit **embarrassed** too as you'd promised your tutor you'd make it this month. You leave a message on her answerphone to reassure her of your continuing commitment.
9.45am	A mother comes up to you complaining about the nursery policy on sickness. She shouts a lot.	The mother is feeling **upset** and scared about getting into trouble at work if she misses another day, but comes across as **angry**. You're initial feeling is one of **anger** at the unfairness of the complaint, but also feel empathy for the parent who had fought hard to get this first job and anxiety for the child who is clearly too sick to be in school. The staff member hovering in the background is **upset** and **angry** and looking to you for support. The child is feeling **scared** and looking anxiously to all the adults.
10.30am	Rabia takes her first steps.	This little girl has had a difficult few months so everyone (including you) is **delighted** and **happy**. You phone the mother (as you'd promised) and she cries on the phone and you listen to her explain how much this means to her, feeling rather emotional yourself. You're suddenly and unexpectedly **glad** that you're covering in baby room today. You're also proud of the staff and the nursery who have worked so hard with this family and the health professionals to help make this moment happen.
11.30am	Lunch is late. Again.	Everyone is complaining, except you who have to manage the situation calmly. You feel **frustrated** that this still happens despite all your efforts and sorry for the children and staff who are kept waiting.
12.30am	The sun comes out.	Children and staff cheer up and go outside to have a picnic with the fruit and cake provided for pudding. You join them and relax and **enjoy** the moment.

Intelligence. Daniel Goleman et al. in the book *The New Leaders* identified five different strands, each with its own competences:

1. **Knowing your emotions**

2. **Managing your own emotions**

3. **Motivating yourself**

4. **Recognising and understanding other people's emotions/motivations**

5. **Managing relationships, i.e. managing the emotions of others.**

If anyone is in any doubt about the importance of emotional intelligence for a leader in early years settings, consider the things that might happen in a typical morning in a nursery, for example the scenario presented on page 16.

What are your strengths?

Everybody has strengths and these are going to be the foundations of any work you do as a leader. Which of these words

do people use to describe you? Resilient, patient, understanding, energetic, creative, passionate, honest, open, fun, positive, reliable, trustworthy, careful, enterprising, thoughtful, kind.

Take some time to think about and list your strengths:

- As a practitioner?

- At home?

- In a crisis?

- With friends?

- Everyday?

Now think about your leadership role and the challenges you face. How can the strengths you have shown in other areas of your life help you with these challenges?

KEY POINTS IN THE REFLECTIVE LEADER

"Seek first to understand and then to be understood" Stephen Covey (1992) *7 Habits of Highly Effective People*.

In this chapter we have focused on how you can use your emotional intelligence to understand yourself more: your goals, intentions, responses, behaviour and feelings. Use your journal to help you continually reflect and build on your strengths. If you are going through a difficult or particularly challenging time, it can be really energising to try writing down, at the end of each day, something that you achieved today and of which you are proud.

In the early years sector I think that we are all too often prone to identifying the things that didn't go so well. We are less good at noticing and celebrating our strengths. As a leader, we may not often have the opportunity to get positive feedback or appreciation from a 'line manager' – we need to do it for ourselves. Talking to a group of practitioners on leadership courses, many found it difficult initially to talk about

what they had done well, what their strengths were. However, when they focused, and helped each other, everyone could find something in their day to celebrate, for example:

- Listening to a parent and helping her to make the first steps for building the confidence to start taking control of her life

- Finding someone to help with the administration

- Finding the time to play with the children in the toddler room – and finding out how much more confident and creative the room leader is becoming

- Reading a story with a new child and parent, and feeling the beginnings of rapport

- Sorting out snack time

- Opening my data file – tomorrow I'll actually read it!

Chapter 3

Where are we going? The importance of vision

"Make sure you know where you are going – as a man who is going nowhere usually gets there!" Unknown Author.

"Go confidently in the direction of your dreams. Live the life you've imagined" Henry David Thoreau.

What is a vision? Why does it matter?

Your vision is central to your role as a leader. It is the better place you are taking your setting towards. It is both a standard of excellence to aspire to, and the purpose of current work. At its best, it binds and motivates the team and provides energy to get the job done. It provides meaning and purpose to all the work of the setting. A vision, then, is not a thing to be lightly plucked from the air. It has to resonate with and be owned by the whole community, providing common goals and shared values. It needs to be connected to the present, but provide inspiration for a future that is sufficiently different to be challenging, but practical enough to be achievable.

Your vision will be informed by your pedagogy and your values, your knowledge of the setting and the needs of the community. You may have been inspired by another setting or an experience in your own education. Where you start and what you might do in identifying and elaborating your vision will vary hugely depending on your individual situation. You may need to start from scratch with a new vision or you may already have a vision.

What is your vision?

Take some time to think about your vision, what you want to achieve for your setting. If you already have a vision for your setting, write it down in your learning journal and ask yourself these questions:

- Does it describe a better future?

| Is that future consistent with high standards for quality and outcomes for children?

| Is it a vision that everybody in the setting can connect with?

| Does it motivate people and help to provide a sense of purpose and direction for your setting?

- Does it connect well with the values and culture of your setting?

- Is it realistic? Are there practical steps that you can take to work towards the vision?

Letter from the future

If you don't already have a vision, or you are finding it difficult to clarify your thoughts, you might find this exercise from the world of coaching useful, interesting and fun.

Imagine that it is some time in the future, maybe next year or the year after. Someone somewhere has waved a magic wand and everything you ever dreamed of for your setting has come true. That might mean that you have had the time and opportunity to build on your strengths, or perhaps to tackle a concern.

Imagine yourself walking into your setting that day in the future. What are you feeling as you open the door? As you walk in through the door, what does it feel like? What do you see and hear? What are the children doing, and the parents? What do they say to you as you arrive? Now look at the staff, what are they doing? How are they interacting with the children and the parents? What do they say to you about their work in the setting? Finally, what are you doing in the setting, what do you say, think, feel about your work.

Practice examples of vision

What vision do you have for your setting?

Velda

Velda's initial inspiration for her pre-school was to recreate the supportive family atmosphere of the nursery her children used to go to. However, the practicalities of running a business with budgets to balance, premises to manage and policies to write had taken up increasingly large amounts of her time and energy and the vision had got a little left behind. When Ofsted rated the setting only 'satisfactory' Velda and the team felt demoralised and unsure what to do. They had all worked so hard. A visit to a friend's happy and successful nursery and a frank discussion with an enthusiastic local adviser helped to re-energise Velda's passion. She talked to the team about her dream of creating a warm, creative nursery, at the heart of the community. Thinking about a positive future helped the staff regain their energy and remember what had inspired them to join Velda at her nursery in the first place. They all had ideas to contribute and practical suggestions for moving the nursery forward. In sharing her vision with her team, Velda not only empowered them, but found the support and encouragement she needed to start to realise her dream.

Henry

Henry hadn't expected to become the foundation stage leader when the position became vacant in only his third year of teaching. However he was enthusiastic, energetic and the head was impressed with his EYFSP results so he got the job. The deputy was very supportive. He made time for Henry to talk about what he wanted for the school's foundation stage and also helped him to plan meetings where the whole team could contribute their thoughts on what was important too. What emerged was a very strong, shared commitment to listening to the child's voice and a desire to use this to inform a more sensitive and responsive planning system.

Another key area that emerged for the vision in this setting was to create a positive learning environment for everyone – staff and children – where risks were encouraged and mistakes seen as opportunities for further learning. Henry recognised that this was going to be essential if the staff were going to be freed-up to genuinely try out the new, more flexible way of working with the children.

Lydia's Letter

Dear Lydia,

I am still working at Crossacres, but you wouldn't recognise it now. We have changed the entrance so that it is a comfortable place for parents to come into with the children, with lots of leaflets and ideas of things to do, some of them in community languages. We've also got a board up with photographs of the children and parents at one of our workshops, with lots of comments from the parents too, all positive.

The main room is still the same long, thin shape, but we have made the space much more enclosed for the children using trolleys and display boards to create a series of 'mini-rooms'. It feels a much more relaxing place to be for children and adults.

Our planning has changed a lot. We still follow the children's interests and development, but we've got better at thinking of really interesting things to provide for the children to take those interests on – this week we've got snow and ice from the garden in the water tray and the children are doing experiments using sand timers to find out how quickly they can get bits to melt. All this means that when you walk in through the door you first notice how much quieter it is, and you hardly see the staff as they're all playing with the children. Oh, and I mustn't forget to tell you about the outdoor space! We've put up a special curtain across the doors to help keep the heat in but the children can go in and out whenever they want: free-flow without being told off by the landlord about electricity bills!

I'm much happier than I was. I'm proud of what we are doing in the community.

All the parents speak well of us and we have a waiting list for places. I spend more time with the children and the staff. It was hard to find time in the beginning but I've found it keeps my energy and enthusiasm much higher and that when I do work with the team it helps to keep us all motivated and thinking about those high standards we are looking for. How did I get there? Well...

Now write a letter to yourself from that time. Describe in your letter what is happening in this magical place in the future, and what you did to get there. That is your 'better place' and that is often a very good place to start looking for your vision. Some people also find it helpful to draw a picture of where they are – turning the letter into a 'postcard'.

If your 'better place' does not feel quite right for you yet, try going on visits to other settings to get your creative juices flowing. Or talk to people you know and trust to remind yourself of your enthusiasms and passions. Put some magazines in the staff room to stimulate talk and discussion. Some people find it helpful to look back at important times in their past when their work has been going particularly well and remind themselves about what was special about that time. Others revisit favourite books, or sign up for some interesting looking courses.

Whatever method works for you, we all need what a colleague of mine once called 'professional oxygen'. We need time to get back in touch with what really matters to us, to learn new things and use that information to keep our vision, our passion and our energy alive.

I recently worked with a group of early years practitioners on a leadership course and we asked them: "What is it that gets you up in the morning? What inspires you about your work?". Without exception, everyone responded with something along the lines of "making a difference for children and families". Yet everyone in this same group also felt that they had to make a real effort to spend time on this area of their work and that "paperwork" and "bureaucracy" frequently pulled them away from what really mattered to them, what had drawn them into working in early years in the first place.

With the EYFS putting a real emphasis on the importance of spending time with children and recommending a significant reduction in paperwork, this can be a real opportunity to reflect on what matters most in your setting, and how you can make sure that you control your paperwork – rather than letting it control you!

Paperwork

It may seem odd to have a section on paperwork in a chapter on vision, but many of the people I work with put 'paperwork' as one of the main reasons they are not able to find the time and/or motivation to focus on their vision for the setting – and putting that vision into practice, so it seems sensible to address that issue head on!

Most of us chose to work with young children because it attracted us more than working in an office, yet when we take on a leadership role there sometimes feels huge pressure to move away from the children and families and focus instead on 'paperwork'. However much the revised EYFS promises to "reduce bureaucracy" there is always going to be the necessity for some paperwork. One important element of being a successful and happy leader is to find a way to make sure that your paperwork does its job with the maximum efficiency and minimum of time. What is going to be the solution will vary hugely from setting to setting, but here are a few ideas for you to think about and decide which might be helpful for you in your setting.

How can you reduce the time you spend on paperwork?

1. Evaluate the purpose of the paperwork.

2. Paperwork should be there to help you do your job more effectively. That means it helps you remember important information, helps you analyse that information to make decisions and helps you communicates that information effectively and efficiently to others. At the same time, well-kept paperwork provides a useful audit trail for other stakeholders like Ofsted or the nursery owner. When you do your paperwork, think about what the purpose of the paperwork you are doing really is – and if it is fit for that purpose.

3. Have a paperwork audit.

4. Most of us build up systems, processes, policies and files over time and sometimes these duplicate each other or are no longer really necessary. Take time out to review everything (preferably with a friend who is organised and good at detail) and decide what you absolutely need to keep doing, what you can stop doing and what you might like to do differently.

5. Set a timetable.

6. Put time aside each day/week/month (whatever works for you) to do the different aspects of paperwork in short, sharp bursts – and stick to those times. Constantly re-juggling different tasks and priorities saps energy – and wastes time as we have to 'start again' when we forget where we are. If there is no particular time-scale period to complete the forms then many of us find that the task drags on indefinitely.

7. Find a helper.

8. Not just any helper – there are some people who are naturally much more efficient with the detail and process of many aspects of paperwork than others. Use these wonderful people wisely. What can take you a day can sometimes be done by others in an hour. We all have different strengths; if yours is working with people, supporting parents, inspiring staff or creating a wonderful environment then make sure you have the time to do those things.

9. One leader I know says her life has changed by getting someone in to do a small amount of administration each week. Another new leader in a difficult setting has shared out the administrative tasks between the three senior members of the team so that each has a manageable, clearly defined "task" – helping to support leaders for the future as well as giving herself much needed time for working with the team to improve the quality of the provision.

Think about how you manage your paperwork now. Is there something you could stop doing? Is there something you could start doing?

Living the vision

Vision displayed

Once you are clear about your vision, a useful thing you can do to help make sure that your vision resonates throughout your setting is to make it visible in writing. Some settings put something in their prospectus; others put it on their walls. Here is an example from a pre-school kitchen area. They reworked their vision after a period of disruption where many staff were coming and going, identifying a focus on the children as being at the heart of their vision.

> "Our children always come first. Our planning is informed by our knowledge and understanding of the children, their stage of development and their interests. This term we are all working together to improve the quality of our observational assessments and working with parents to introduce learning journeys."

The pre-school manager collected photographs of quality work in action around the nursery that reflected the vision in practice and displayed these around the statement, adding to it as dream and reality became ever closer.

Getting the practitioners you needs means investing time in the recruitment process

Recruiting for the vision

It's also essential to keep your vision firmly in the front of your mind when you are interviewing new staff. If your vision includes open and honest partnerships with parents and a setting at the heart of its community, then that's worth exploring with practitioners coming for interview. As part of a piece of research into team-working I once interviewed the head of Human Resources (HR) of a well-respected high street store to ask them how they always managed to have such helpful and positive sales assistants. His answer was that at interview they always looked for people who shared their values and approach. "You can teach nearly anyone how to sell a radio or a piece of kitchen equipment," he said, "but it's not so easy to teach people to be enthusiastic, positive and respectful of all different kinds of customers – and that's what is really important to us as a company".

Getting the team for the vision

A robust interview process that explores values will help you to recruit the staff you need to make your vision a reality, and will also help you ensure the safety of your children. Think about what the important values are that you will look for in recruiting your staff team? What questions might you ask to find out if they share those values? Here are a few examples:

> Why did you choose to work with young children?

> What motivates and inspires you?

> Tell me about how you like to work with parents…

Use follow-up questions to 'bland' or impersonal answers. For example: "You say you see parents as partners in their children's learning – tell me a little more about how you go about this?" or "can you give me an example of how you have supported a particularly vulnerable parent?".

Encourage practitioners to demonstrate their ability to reflect and learn with questions like "what do you see as your strengths and how do you plan to develop them further?" or "what do you see as your areas for development" followed by "and how are you working on these?".

You might ask: "Having visited our nursery and read our brochure, what stands out for you about what we offer here?" followed by "and how do you see yourself supporting that approach?".

How safe is your recruitment?

1.	Do you have a clear policy that describes who does what and when throughout the process?
2.	Do you have a written safeguarding policy? Are there clear references to your policy in your recruitment documents and different stages of the selection process?
3.	Do you regularly review your job descriptions to make sure that you are recruiting for the posts you really need? How are the job descriptions reflected in the person specifications? Are you confident that you have identified the knowledge, skills, experience, qualifications and attributes that really matter to you?
4.	How do you decide where to advertise in order to reach the most and the best potential candidates? What do you put in your advertisements to really inspire and motivate people to want to come and work with you? How do you make sure that unsuitable candidates are not encouraged to apply?
5.	What do you have in your candidate information pack that is going to make sure your candidates are well informed about the values and quality of your setting? What essential information about the application process do you include that will enable candidates to show themselves at their best?
6.	Who do you have on your shortlisting panel to ensure that each application is given fair and equal consideration? How do you ensure that each application is also rigorously scrutinised to identify any possible concerns that might necessitate removing a candidate from a shortlist? How do you manage internal candidates or candidates proposed by staff already in the setting to make sure that the process is as fair and rigorous for them as for everybody else?
7.	How do you ensure that all appropriate checks are made on your short listed candidates, including following up references? What additional checks might you want to do before offering a candidate a position – and how explicit is it to a candidate when you offer a position, that this is subject to satisfactory checks (e.g. enhanced CRB)?
8.	How to you decide what to include in the interviewing process in order to allow the candidates to show themselves at their best, whilst also enabling the interview panel to probe carefully into the most important aspects of the person specification and the job description, or strengths and weaknesses in the candidate's job history (including gaps)? How much information do you need to give candidates in advance (e.g. if they are going to read a story to a group of children, or prepare an activity to show the panel)?
9.	How do you ensure that an objective decision is reached, based on evidence from a face-to-face interview and other activities?

Personally I always like to see interviewees in real situations so I might ask a practitioner to prepare and read a story to a small group of (confident) children and/or give a group of interviewees a small, practical task to work on together (for example planning a coffee morning for parents or a teddy bears' picnic). The first gives you real information about how they relate to children, and the second how they work in a team with other adults.

Don't be afraid to ask the difficult questions, for example about safeguarding: "What would you do if you were concerned about a child or about a member of staff?".

Safe recruitment

Robust interviewing is only one of the important steps you need to take in order to be confident that you are recruiting staff that will help you keep the children in your setting safe, cared for, learning and developing. Look at the questions below and think about your own recruitment practice. What are your strengths? What might be areas that you need to develop?

Leading and living the vision

As a leader you have an important role to play in making sure that the vision for your setting is part of everyday life. For example, from our case studies on page 19, it would have been important for Velda, if she wanted her vision for a creative setting to come alive, to visibly model this in her setting every day. Perhaps she might lead an activity herself to get things started. Or she might walk the setting everyday noting the opportunities for children to express and develop their creativity and share her thoughts with the team: "That's a wonderful idea to take the books outside today and you're right to think that it would be good to have an enclosed space for them. A den's a great plan too and I think it would really engage the children's creativity if we could get them involved in making the den together". She might also scrutinise the planning and make a comment on a Post-it® when she noted particularly good creative ideas being developed – or areas where more creativity would be helpful.

As foundation stage leader, Henry was also a reception class teacher and might use this to help lead the vision, sharing his

POINT FOR REFLECTION

How is the experience of first time visitors to your school? What does it say about your vision? What do the signs say? What might visitors feel when they read them (one children's centre I visited had antiseptic hand lotion outside to rub on your hands – I wondered if some visitors might feel 'unclean')? How easy is it to find the way through to a reception area (if you have one)? What's the experience when you reach reception? Do the people in reception know how to acknowledge and greet visitors whilst also dealing with a phone call or busy reception area? How do you find out what the visitor experience is like? Do you ask parents, new members of staff, governors or committee members for feedback?

planning with the other staff, perhaps increasing the amount of joint planning across the team. This would enable him to demonstrate the process of his planning as well as the detail of the experiences and activities he put into practice in his classroom.

For example, he might explain how he had tried to capture the voice of a newly-arrived child who didn't speak very much, by watching her closely and thinking about what her behaviour was telling him about her interests, needs, thoughts and skills. Henry might then go on to ask the other members of the team for their view on what they thought might be happening for this little girl. He might ask what other experiences he could offer that they thought would better meet her developmental needs and take forward her thoughts and interests. By so doing he would be living his vision even more accurately, showing his team that he didn't expect to get it right first time, that there would always be learning to do, and that he valued their insights and views on how to think about the children and planning for their needs in a more responsive way.

It is also important to ask for feedback about how closely you are getting to your vision from people outside the immediate team, as Crystal, the leader of a busy foundation stage in a large primary school said recently: "I need people to come in from outside with new eyes. I know that sometimes I only see what I think is happening, not what is really there".

At the heart of Crystal's vision was a close partnership with parents from all members of the community. She had fought for

and achieved funding to enable every new child to have a home visit. The reception area was bright and welcoming, reflecting the rich diversity of the local community through the languages used and the pictures displayed. The team regularly organised social and educational workshops and visits, including a trip to the local park and a coffee meeting with a local speech therapist. What she didn't know, until she'd asked a friend from another school to visit the school as a 'mystery shopper' was that the first impressions created by the entry into the school were totally out of alignment with her vision of welcome and warmth.

The entrance to nursery and reception was through a small door cut into a high brick wall. Beside the door was a sign that said: 'Visitors to nursery and reception press here for entry'. Having pressed the buzzer the door would be released and the visitor would find themselves in a small tarmac courtyard with a door the other side. At this door there was another buzzer and a sign 'Press for entry'. This time when the door opened the visitor would find herself in the attractive reception area, with an office to one side. The office staff would finish what they were doing and ask the visitor's name and business and get them to sign in the visitor book and issue a pass.

Crystal's friend explained that whilst the system worked efficiently, it all felt very cold and formal, and was probably rather daunting to someone visiting the school for the first time, especially anyone who was not fluent in written English. As they talked about it and reflected some more, Crystal wondered if that might be one of the reasons why some local families were choosing a more distant school.

The importance of next steps

A vision remains a dream, unless you as the leader, can help your team to identify and put into action the next step that will take you closer to making that dream a reality. The feedback that Crystal got from her 'mystery shopper' was unexpected and challenging. It was unexpected, as no-one in the school experienced that 'first impression'. It was challenging because initially Crystal felt constrained by both the architecture of the building and health and safety requirements. However, she also felt that 'doing nothing' was not an option as it was becoming increasingly clear to her that the first impression was probably putting off some of the families she most wanted to encourage to the school.

Initially, Crystal could not see the 'answer' to the overall problem, but discussing with her friend and her colleagues

Bringing the vision to life

Your vision and mission statement are not just pieces of paper; they are also ways of being for adults and children

In a large setting that combined a nursery school and children's centre, the head was concerned that her vision was not 'taking off' as she had thought and hoped it would. Progress in some key areas had stalled and she sensed tensions between different groups of staff. She organised a team day for all members of staff where everyone was supported and encouraged to talk frankly about their work in a safe environment – the priorities, the rewards and the challenges.

Staff responded with enthusiasm, and everyone began to realise what the issue was. The vision and values statement had become a 'piece of paper' that was not meaningful any more to the people working there. It had been drawn up before the children's centre was established and everyone had assumed that it would cover the new services and people. The honest and open discussions in the team day revealed that the staff working in the children's centre were more concerned at this stage in increasing their "reach" into the community, making positive relationships with the many different aspects of the community and encouraging them to use the centre by providing a very "client" led offer. The nursery school, on the other hand with many years of

outstanding practice to its credit, retained the idea of making sure that the very best possible quality provision was at the heart of its vision and purpose.

Bringing the differences into the light and providing a safe place to talk about them was liberating and energising. It took some challenging but rewarding work with all members of staff to clarify priorities and values and agree a vision that everyone could sign up to which focused on improving outcomes for children: providing outstanding teaching and learning opportunities and making sure that those opportunities were reaching the children and families most in need.

The next step was to involve parents and carers from across the community. The school held informal craft and baking sessions that were popular with the community to provide a time and place to talk about the centre's work. The head also worked with the chair of governors to plan an "away day" for governors to reflect on vision and values in the centre. By the time the vision and mission statement had been agreed and put on the wall in the entrance to the centre, it was something that everybody recognised and could relate to.

What are your first steps towards making your vision a reality?

Putting a man on the moon

There is a (probably apocryphal) story about a visit that John F. Kennedy made to Nassau, at the height of the space race, that sums up for me the purpose and value of having an inspirational vision that is shared by all members of the community. The story goes like this…

> Kennedy was visiting the space station and had talked with many of the astronauts and scientists. He'd talked to the managers and the engineers and had lunch with the directors of the space programme. Before he left he went into the office where the administrators were busy at work with paper.
>
> "Nice to meet you," said the great man, "great place this. Everyone's so busy, working so hard. Can you tell me what your job is?". They could have said: "Typing letters, filing reports, writing cheques and answering the phone". They could have said: "Making sure that the communications work well and that the money adds up". What they said was: "We're putting a man on the moon".

I heard that story just before I took up my first headship and it struck me as an important thing to remember about the role of a leader in providing staff with meaningful purpose and direction, about setting high ideals that everyone could relate to, about encouraging optimism for a better future and connecting us all to a shared culture and values.

helped her to see some useful "first steps" which could help to take the school closer to her vision. She redesigned the signs to include welcoming pictures and used words like 'welcome' in more than one language (initially these were on laminated card). The premises manager painted coloured footprints on the ground, from the gate to the reception door. The office staff all agreed to greet visitors from the moment they came through the door and to talk to them first before doing the official business of signing-in and getting the badge.

KEY POINTS IN WHERE ARE WE GOING? THE IMPORTANCE OF VISION

In this chapter we have thought about the importance of having a shared vision for a better future, where that might come from and how to work towards achieving it, including how to recruit staff who can share your vision and your values. Your vision is one of the most powerful tools you have for motivating yourself and others. A strong, well-articulated vision is also essential for external communications with parents, governors, committees, owners and Ofsted. How could you articulate your vision to someone else in three simple sentences?

Chapter 4

Building a team

"*Alone we can do so little; together we can do so much*"
Helen Keller, early 20th century author and activist who was
both deaf and blind.

Nobody can implement a vision on their own, no matter how
powerful the vision or how energetic the leader. In order to
share and develop your vision for a better setting, you need to
have practitioners that are positive, enthused and committed
and share your vision. A good starting point is to build on your
effective recruitment with clear policy and practice around
induction of new staff. As it says in the revised EYFS at 3.18:
"*The daily experience of children in early years settings and the
overall quality of provision depends on all practitioners having
appropriate qualifications, training, skills and knowledge and a
clear understanding of their roles and responsibilities. Providers
must ensure that all practitioners receive induction training to
help them understand their roles and responsibilities*".

Induction of new staff

How you induct your staff will vary according to the particular
needs of your setting. However, the following list of suggestions –
gathered from a range of different settings, is a helpful reference
point when considering what works best for you and your team:

- Each new member of staff is assigned a mentor, in addition
  to a line manager, who will act as a guide and support during
  the first six months. A mentor (or "buddy") will meet regularly
  with the new staff member to go through documents, explain
  practice and be a first point of call for advice and information
  to ensure that the new recruit settles quickly into the routines
  of the setting. Wherever possible it is helpful for mentors to
  have some training to support them in this important role.

| All the setting policies are collected into a single folder with
  a brief synopsis in the front explaining the purpose and remit
  of each. The line-manager or mentor goes through this with

Providers need to ensure that all new staff have induction
training to help them settle quickly into the life of the setting

the new member of staff before starting work. The EYFS
emphasises the importance of new practitioners being clear
about emergency evacuation procedures, safeguarding,
child protection, equality policy and health and safety issues.

- In addition, each member of staff has a copy of the 'staff
  handbook' which provides more practical day-to-day
  information about the operational activities of the setting; for
  example, models of planning and assessment, timetables, lists
  of staff and their responsibilities, where equipment is kept, key
  phone numbers, procedures for staff absence, tea and coffee
  money, social activities etc. Again, this is far more useful if a

member of staff takes the time to go through it with the new practitioner, answering questions and filling in any gaps.

- On their first morning, the setting leader accompanies the new practitioner to introduce her/him to all other members of staff – for this reason it is sometimes a good idea to choose a start time when there is likely to more capacity and therefore time. A calm start can really help to ensure that the new member of staff not only has all the information needed, but also begins to pick up and internalise the working ethos of the setting.

- Have a list of important 'firsts' that are ticked off during the first year and make sure that either the line manager or the mentor goes through them in detail with the new practitioner as they arise. It is usually too much to take in at the start of a job, and is easily forgotten if the knowledge is not to be used for several months. The sorts of things that fit into this list are the first Christmas Party, outings, parents' evening, reports, governors' meeting or committee, end of term and visitors. These are things with a mass of detail that a setting can often take for granted that everyone knows. I remember one new practitioner in a setting who was chastised by a member of the management committee for sitting in the wrong chair at an event – but no-one had explained the sensitivities around seating to her!

Providing ongoing support for staff

The supportive, or enabling, role of a leader, continues beyond the induction period for all staff. In addition to providing an enabling environment for our children, we need to think about what an enabling environment might look like for our practitioners. We need to provide the kind of supportive work environment where all practitioners can feel positive about themselves and their work.

LINKS WITH YOUR PRACTICE

If you don't already have an induction policy, or want to update it, think about how to involve all your current staff in this process. You may wish to have a free-discussion session where everybody feels confident about contributing their own ideas and then you (or someone you delegate this to if you have a large team) could take away all the ideas and work up a first draft. Alternatively, if you think that your staff might find that too unstructured, you could try to complete a first draft yourself and then give it to the rest of the team to read and comment and make suggestions.

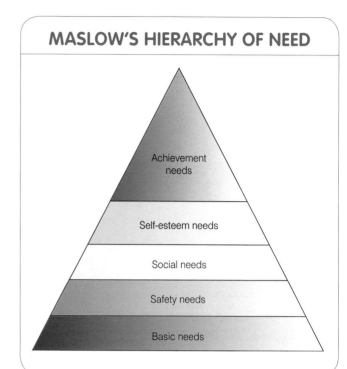

MASLOW'S HIERARCHY OF NEED

- Achievement needs
- Self-esteem needs
- Social needs
- Safety needs
- Basic needs

You may be familiar with Maslow's Hierarchy of Need from your study of child development. We know that the young children in our care cannot focus on learning if, for example, they are tired, hungry or anxious. Children need to have their basic, safety and social needs met before they can focus on their self-esteem and achievement needs. The same applies to us as adults. It can be a useful exercise to work through the different levels of need, reflecting on where your team is on this hierarchy at the moment.

Do your practitioners have regular breaks, with the opportunity to eat and drink sufficiently to function in a lively pre-school setting? Is the temperature comfortable? Does your dress code mean that all your practitioners are dressed appropriately for working outside in the colder months? In the hotter months we always have water available for children, but do we also make sure that our practitioners are keeping hydrated too?

Safety needs

Most early years settings are scrupulous about their attention to health and safety for both children and adults. For adults, there are other safety needs that sometimes need thinking about that don't come under the 'health and safety' badge. For example, practitioners on temporary contracts or probation may feel very anxious about their position in a way that is restricting their creativity and playfulness with the children. Whilst we can't always agree the contract our practitioners want, it is helpful to make sure that our paperwork for contracts is up-to-date and regularly reviewed, and that practitioners on probation or training are given regular, honest feedback on their progress. And every manager knows that the fastest way to staff discord is through getting the pay wrong; if practitioners can't be confident about what they will be taking home at the end of the week, it leads directly to feelings of insecurity and unease.

Settings that have a no-blame approach to mistakes are supporting practitioners' sense of safety and security. It is much easier to try out new ideas, or admit to something going wrong if you know that the issue is going to be discussed objectively without recourse to blame, anger or personal criticism. On the other hand, practitioners that work in fear of making a mistake and 'being told off' are not in a good place to develop their professional practice beyond just 'getting through the day'.

Another important aspect of meeting safety and security needs as a manager is choosing how much information to share with the rest of the team; and when we do decide to share it, choosing how to express that information so as to minimise feelings of anxiety. For example, the head of a large nursery had an Ofsted inspection recently. At the end of the morning the head met the staff in two groups to give them brief feedback on how it was going so far. What she had been told was that the inspector was looking at a 'satisfactory' or even an 'inadequate' judgement. What she told the staff was that she knew they'd had a difficult start to the day, but that she knew they could get 'good' and that they should be proud and confident in what they did. The setting did get a good, and afterwards the head told her team about the negative start to the inspection. They were amazed and gave her some heartfelt feedback: "You could never have told that you'd just had that bad news – you were brilliant and totally motivated us all for the rest of the day!".

Social needs

Practitioners need to feel that they 'belong' within the setting, that they are appreciated and are part of a team. Managers often support practitioners in this way by introducing small social moments into the life of the settings, perhaps bringing in cakes to celebrate a birthday or organising a team outing at the end of term. Most settings have notice boards with photos of all members of staff. Some managers have found it helpful to have a planned induction for all new members of staff (including students), with a handbook with useful information about policies, timetables etc. and perhaps a 'buddy' or mentor to provide personal support

> ## POINT FOR REFLECTION
>
> What is your induction policy for new members of staff? How do you make sure it is always up to date and relevant?
>
> How do you support your staff with their different needs? Is there anybody on the team who you think might be feeling insecure? Or who is not being given the opportunity to develop their full potential? How do you regularly show appreciation for your team? Is there anyone on the team who might be feeling a bit 'left out' – perhaps because they are new, or a little older or younger than other members of the team?

during the first weeks. Some teams meet regularly outside the setting, strengthening the sense of belonging to the team.

Self-esteem needs

As managers, one of the most important ways that we support our staff with their development of self-esteem is by making sure that we observe all members of the team working in the setting regularly, recognising and praising effort and achievement. Several managers I have met say they begin and end every day walking round the setting greeting each practitioner personally to show their appreciation. Some settings have an 'employee of the week', others have a notice board where they share success stories. In one large day nursery I visited there was a board in the kitchen where the busy manager found time to put up comments every day about what she saw and appreciated in her nursery. In that same nursery, the photos of the members of staff had captions next to them, each saying something important about the practitioner, for example what languages they spoke, or that they were responsible for the new library area.

Achievement needs

I strongly believe that at heart, everybody is motivated to want to do well. Nobody gets up in the morning and says to themselves: "I want to be a miserable, low achieving member of the team". People naturally want to do a good job, whatever it might look like on the surface. (Remember the Johari Window from Chapter 2? What your practitioners present to you might not be the whole story of what is going on for them. Many people hide feelings of insecurity or worries about failure under an outward display of indifference or aggression.)

Think of a time when you were feeling highly motivated. What were you doing? How was the task or project presented to you? How much choice did you have over what you did and how you did it? Who else was involved? What were they doing? How did you feel when you were engaged in the task? How did you feel when you had achieved what you set out to do (if you did)?

Now think of a time where you were feeling highly demotivated and answer the same questions above.

What does this tell you about what kinds of tasks/experiences motivate you?

What does it tell you about how you like your tasks to be presented and supported?

As managers we can help support the achievement needs of our practitioners through providing good quality continuing professional development (CPD), encouraging an ethos of learning for adults, as well as children. Performance management or supervision meetings are an excellent opportunity to talk to practitioners about their ambitions, hopes and aspirations and to discuss how you, as the manager, can best support them. Interestingly, psychologists tell us that easy goals are not motivating, so it is worth exploring with your practitioners just how far they can go – who would like to take on responsibility for a curriculum area? Or plan a parents' evening? Or choose and design a new role play area?

Motivation

Understanding our hierarchy of needs can help bring us insights into human motivation, what drives us. Maslow's theory is that if our basic needs are met, then all human beings will be motivated to meet their "achievement needs".

X and Y theories of motivation

Understanding and meeting practitioner need is an important part of our role in motivating staff. Another key aspect of our ability to motivate staff is to be found in our deeply held beliefs about people and their attitude to work. What we believe affects our behaviour; how we treat people and that changes the motivation that practitioners have for their work.

As Richard Olivier wrote in his inspirational book on leadership based on Shakespeare's Henry V:

> "We will always tend to lead others the way we want to be led, but until we understand what truly motivates others we will be unable to appeal to their following effectively" from Inspirational Leadership, p.63.

We all have different ways we approach change or challenge, have different feelings about risk taking and experimentation or about independence or collaborative working. Whilst we may work in a setting where we share a pedagogy/philosophy about how children learn, different practitioners will also have different passions – such as for outdoor learning or art and design. They may be wildly enthusiastic about working with parents but only moderately excited by the development of children's phonological awareness. On the other hand, they may be much more comfortable with working with children at "table top" activities and feel awkward or unconfident on the floor with free-flow block play.

As leaders we will work with all practitioners and all aspects of early learning, but we will have our own individual commitments to different aspects of our work. And it is the very diversity of skills, talents and knowledge that make a great team. Understanding the complexity of that diversity also means that we will need to understand and support different motivational needs. What motivates a young, confident practitioner straight out of college may be different from what motivates your deputy with 30 years of service behind her and a complex family to support. As a leader it is important to know what really motivates your individual, unique members of staff and build on them. The best way to find out about your staff is to listen and in the next chapter we will explore what professional listening might look like when we are working with staff.

Psychologists tell us that as well the individual motivations that come from personal passions, there are similarities in the human psyche that can help us as managers tune-in to our practitioners and help them develop to be the best they can be. Writing in the 1960s, Douglas McGregor suggested that there are two fundamentally different approaches to managing people that he called **Theory X** and **Theory Y**. He noticed that many managers tended towards theory X, and generally got poor results. Enlightened managers, on the other hand, held to theory Y, which produced better performance and results, allowing people to grow and develop to their full potential. Many of us will have memories of having been managed by someone who (often subconsciously) holds to Theory X. Fortunately in the Early Years, most of us instinctively lean towards Theory Y which mirrors so closely our beliefs about how young children learn. Jenny Rogers in her excellent book, *Adults Learning*, describes the two theories as follows:

"People who lead, manage or teach using 'Theory X' assumptions believe that human beings cannot be trusted to work. They believe that we will avoid responsibility and effort if we can, therefore we must be controlled, directed, manipulated, force-fed and punished for disobedience. A more benign version of this style is also possible, characterised by condescension and faint praise, but where power and control are still essentially with the leader.

Theory Y leaders believe the opposite: that work is natural and that we work best when we take responsibility for ourselves. Creativity and play are important for problem solving and the only way to do this is through engaging people, trusting them and giving them autonomy. Praise is more effective than criticism as a way to lead".

Believing that people naturally want to do a good job and that believing in them and giving them space to make their own decisions and result in better practice, is not the easy option.

It is often difficult to keep on believing in our staff at the end of a difficult few weeks where nothing seems to be going right and the new member of the team keeps coming in late and upsetting the rota. Sometimes, as Michael Fullan says in *The Moral Imperative Realised*, we need to respect our staff before they have earned it. Sometimes our respecting them is the first step to them respecting themselves. In his earlier book, *The Moral Imperative of School Leadership*, Fullan made another important statement about motivation that clearly puts him in the Theory Y box when he says:

"There is no greater motivator than internal accountability to oneself and ones peers. It makes for a better profession, and it makes for a better system".

I remember talking to one young practitioner who said that her experience at school had been nearly entirely negative. She had no self-confidence and when she first started working this often came across as being moody and lethargic. She said that the praise she got from her manager for getting the first little things right made all the difference. She started seeing herself for the first time as someone who could be successful – and successful she became.

POINT FOR REFLECTION

Have you ever been managed by someone who had a Theory X style? What did if feel like? How motivated were you to work? What was the impact on your practice?

Have you ever been managed by someone who had a Theory Y style? What did that feel like? How different was your motivation and the impact on your practice?

Think about your own practice. Most of us in the early years will naturally tend towards a Theory Y style, but under pressure may find that we are subconsciously adopting a more Theory X approach. When might that happen for you? What is the impact on staff morale and motivation?

What motivates your staff to be the best they can be?

Delegation

If you talk to practitioners about motivation, one of the things they will commonly cite as a reason for feeling demotivated is poor delegation practice on the part of their manager. Delegation is hard work on both sides. It requires a high level of trust, excellent communication skills and a culture where people are free to try things out and make mistakes without being penalised. There are a number of common ways where delegation can be less successful than it should:

> **Where people think they have delegated, but have not really 'let go'.**

This is a hard one and very common. We're really busy, someone offers to help and you delegate a task you think they have time and knowledge to do. However, subconsciously you still feel this is 'your' project. What you have done is not 'delegated' the task, but given it to your colleague hoping that they will do exactly what you would have done – a 'guess what's in my head' exercise that is doomed to failure.

I know just what I'm talking about here as only this year I did exactly that myself. I was feeling overwhelmed with tasks and

How do you delegate a task like putting up a new display?

about to take the first week holiday for eight months. There was a brochure nearly finished that just needed a couple of bits doing before it went to press. I asked a colleague to pick up the work for me and she very kindly agreed. However, I had lived with this brochure for weeks. I'd poured over the copy, spent hours choosing pictures, weeks with the designer and in my heart I was still wanted to make those final decisions. So I found a way to be in touch with my colleague and the designer and proceeded to exasperate them both with my well-meaning but intensely irritating interventions. I hadn't really delegated the task at all. I just couldn't do it. I was too emotionally attached to the project.

> **When we're giving a set of instructions a robot could follow.**

Meaningful delegation should involve the delegation of a whole task where the person delegated to has real responsibility to work on something that is challenging and stretching.

An example of an instruction posing as delegation might be telling your deputy that they are in charge tomorrow and writing out all the things that are happening with specific instructions on what they are to say and do for each one. "Mary's mum is coming in at 9.00am to talk about when she's going full-time and I've decided that..., so you will say...Then at 11.00am there's a planning meeting and here's the agenda and I want you to tell everybody..." and so on. This is not delegation; it's trying to do a job by remote control!

> **Delegating something that's been sitting on your desk for weeks because you just couldn't see how to do it – and of course with little time and no budget the colleague you've delegated it to can't do it either.**

I know we would never do this on purpose, but sometimes we might delegate something to someone out of sheer frustration, without thinking through first whether what we are delegating is actually a doable task or not. When it goes wrong we tend to think that it's something to do with delegation, whereas it's not – it's the task itself that is the problem.

Delegation that works

So, given that delegation is so difficult, why do we do it? There are two main reasons:

You can't do everything yourself. You will suffer enormous stress and not be able to get your job done.

One of your roles as a leader is to develop your staff. If you don't delegate effectively, you are denying your practitioners the opportunity to learn and develop their own skills.

Fortunately there are a few tried and tested techniques to help us learn how to effectively delegate so that we reduce our own stress whilst supporting the development of our teams.

Give people a whole task wherever possible: e.g. a complete project; total responsibility for how they plan a day; a complete policy document to develop and consult on.

Be very clear about the level of authority you are giving the other person: how much freedom do they have to act independently without coming back to you? If you have delegated the staff rota to your deputy, at what point might you want her to refer back to you – not at all? If staff are complaining? If parents are complaining? If there is an issue over ratios?

Agree when and how you will check on progress (although you have delegated the task or project you will still be the person ultimately responsible for seeing that it is done, and done to the necessary standard). Will it be a quick chat in the kitchen or will you have an agreed time for a proper discussion? Will you want an update on how the profiles are developing every day, every week, every month?

Be absolutely clear that you want the other person to come to you with any problems they think they can't handle – before the problems become crises. This is not easy – as you don't want to imply to the person to whom you are delegating, that you have any doubts about their competence. You can help by pointing out that the best laid plans can go wrong sometimes and that if they do you will be there to help them sort it out – calmly and with patience. If they think that you will get upset or angry they are more likely to hide problems from you.

How will you and the person you have delegated to, know that the task has been done to the quality that you expect? It helps to set very clear objectives, and to talk to the practitioner about what the completed work might look like, sound like, feel like. For example: "I would like us to have a rota that will always meet essential ratios, even over break times, and will take into consideration staff needs without being dictated by them. It will have extra staff available to be flexible at the start of the day when parents might need to talk to individual members of staff. It will always put the needs of the children first, so will take careful note of the individual needs of children and their key

persons. It will be prepared at least X days in advance and be clearly on display for everybody".

When you delegate the task, be very clear about what time there is available, what resources there are and what the final deadline is. Also check with the person you are delegating to (and yourself!) that the resources you are able to provide (including time) are adequate for the task.

Belbin's theory

Meredith Belbin was a management consultant, whose theory on the importance of respecting and drawing on different strengths and styles in a team has been hugely influential since the early 1980s. He identified a set of nine roles (described briefly on page 34).

His theory was that the best teams have input from all nine, with some team members holding more than one role. This is a particularly important point for us to consider in the early years – where we often have very small teams. In an ideal world, people make the most positive contributions to their teams when they can have a role that fits naturally with their own preferences and style.

For this theory, it is important to remember that there are no 'good' or 'bad' roles. People are as they are, and all roles play important parts in successful teams.

POINT FOR REFLECTION

● In a very small team, how do we identify the different strengths in ourselves and our team members?

l How do we develop our own confidence and resourcefulness in more than one area?

l And how do we support and encourage the same development in others?

Building a team

BELBIN'S NINE ROLES

Role name	Strengths and styles – does 'what' and 'when' throughout the process
Coordinator	Coordinators are confident, calm administrators who are able to pull people together and get them working towards a shared aim.
Shaper	These energetic and highly motivated team members are very focused on results. They will want to make things happen, and can often be very competitive.
Plant	Plants tend to be the creative, problem solving members of a team. They are usually highly innovative, inventive and creative.
Monitor-evaluator	The role of the monitor-evaluator in a team is to bring logical, objective thinking to decision making. They tend to be cautious and analytical thinkers.
Implementer	The implementers in a team tend to be the people who can be most relied on to carry out the work carefully and efficiently. They are highly dependable and loyal, with a great deal of common sense.
Resource investigator	The resource-investigators are the outgoing networkers in the team who look for and find different possibilities and options for action. They tend to be excellent communicators.
Team worker	Highly supportive, sociable and flexible, the team workers have a calming influence on the work of the team. They are usually very perceptive, good listeners and talented mediators.
Completer-finisher	With high standards of quality and an excellent attention to detail, the completer-finisher can be relied on to get things done well and on time.
Specialist	Most teams also need a technical expert who is dedicated to their personal area of expertise and is highly focused on skills and knowledge of their subject area.

KEY POINTS IN TEAM BUILDING

In this chapter we have looked at how understanding motivation can help to build and develop a team.

Also, how motivation may be different for different people, and the benefits of having a diverse team with complementary strengths.

● What do you do in your setting to motivate your team?

I What other things might you do to ensure that everybody feels secure, valued and respected?

I What tasks to you tend to delegate most to your team and how effective is your delegation?

I What areas of team building might you want to develop in your setting?

Chapter 5

An introduction to supervision

"Providers must put appropriate arrangements in place for the supervision of staff who have contact with children and families. Effective supervision provides support, coaching and training for the practitioner and promotes the interests of children. Supervision should foster a culture of mutual support, teamwork and continuous improvement which encourages the confidential discussion of sensitive issues" EYFS 2012.

The requirement for all practitioners to have effective supervision was one of the new parts of the revised 2012 EYFS and grew out of two different issues in the sector:

1. That the sector needs to become more active for developing practice that best meets the needs of the children through putting the responsibility on providers themselves. Quality improvement is no longer to be seen as something that a local authority or government manage. This is an excellent example of Michael Fullan's internal accountability to peers referred to in the last chapter being put into practice.

2. That the sector needs to find ways to protect itself from the kind of horrific safeguarding issues highlighted in the Plymouth Serious Case Review (March 2010) over the allegations of children being sistematically abused by a member of staff, despite the long standing (but unaired) misgivings of other members of staff. The imperative here is to ensure that all members of staff have a safe place in which they can raise sensitive, confidential and potentially disturbing issues – knowing that they will be dealt with appropriately by someone they can trust.

The word **supervision** may be new to many of us. It is a term more routinely used in the health service and social care. We may be more familiar with terms such as 'performance management', 'appraisal' or 'reviews' which, although different from supervision, have areas in common. For example, the key purpose of all these activities is to deliver an improved service to our clients: the children and families with which we work. Because of this important accountability to the people our settings are set up to serve, the supervisor, however supportive, cannot ever suspend critical judgement.

At the same time, without a strong degree of trust and rapport between the supervisor and the supervisee, the relationship will never be able to create the safe environment needed to explore the most difficult areas of a supervisee's work, where she or he feels most vulnerable. When that happens, supervision can either become essentially an paper exercise where the supervisor and supervisee talk on the surface about safe, easy or uncomplicated issues in order to 'tick' the box of having had supervision, or the conversation becomes a defensive confrontation. Neither is healthy or productive.

Supervision is not a paper exercise – it's about improving the service we offer to children and their families

POINT FOR REFLECTION

What have been your own experiences of being supervised (or similar)? What were your expectations and were they met? How did it help the development of your practice? What were the most positive aspects of the process? How could it have been improved?

Supervision can therefore be seen to be a complex activity that draws on many different skills and strengths from the supervisor, the supervisee and the organisation in which it sits. When it works, however, supervision can be one of the most exciting and rewarding aspects of our professional life. It provides the supervisee with the opportunity to stand back from everyday work and reflect on what she or he does, bringing greater objectivity and insights to our everyday work.

Davys and Beddoe in their very helpful book, *Best Practice in Professional Supervision* (2010) draw our attention to the list of characteristics of effective supervision below. I have adapted these for the early years sector. It was drawn from participants on their course. They explain that this list is neither definitive nor exhaustive, but rather is a reflection "of the complexity of this very personal professional practice."

1. **It is an interpersonal, negotiated relationship in which both parties have rights and responsibilities.** If supervision is going to work it is essential that both the supervisee and the supervisor have had a chance to talk through how the supervision relationship can best work for both.

2. **It is accountable – to the organisation, the profession and to the service user.** The main aim of supervision is always to provide a better service for children and their families; to improve the quality of the provision to ensure the safety of all children and to support their learning and development.

3. **It is ethical.** Supervision is essentially a positive, learning activity, focused on providing the supervisee with the right support and challenge in order to maximise their potential. It is a relationship based on mutual respect and trust.

4. **It is confidential.** It is essential that supervision conversations are confidential. Without this, supervisees are

Supervision works best in a setting where everyone is always learning – together

likely to withhold information that they think might put them at risk of censure. In addition, in situations where supervisees might have legitimate concerns about other members of staff that they want to raise, then they are less likely to do so and a chance to prevent a risk to a child may be lost.

5. **It is ongoing and regular – a process rather than an event.** Supervision works best when set within a culture of ongoing learning and development. This means that staff feel encouraged and supported to acquire new skills and knowledge and try them out in the setting – feeling secure that their efforts will be supported and any initial difficulties will be seen as opportunities for further learning, not as a 'failure'. Supervision cannot work effectively in a culture where 'blame' is a common occurrence.

6. **It has boundaries.** Supervision is supportive and personal. It is essential that supervisees have the opportunity during supervision to explore the sometimes difficult emotions that working with children and families can trigger. One of my colleagues recently recounted a story to me of a setting where practitioners used to find excuses to "go into the milk room" just to find the space and time to manage

the emotions they were struggling to deal with in the baby room. In another setting the room leader was exhausted by the emotional strain of supporting parents through some very difficult personal circumstances. Supervision is an ideal forum to raise and discuss the feelings that are raised in our work. The difficult work of the supervisor is to provide a safe place to explore and learn how to manage these feelings professionally so that it is both supportive and challenging. Good listening skills can help to encourage openness and honesty, and good questioning and feedback skills can be helpful in working with supervisees to develop more self-awareness and collaborative problem solving. These are explored in more detail later in this chapter.

7. **It has power dynamics – you are often the line manager.** As we have already discussed, an honest, respectful and trusting relationship is the best foundation for all supervision work. It also needs to be underpinned by a clear supervision contract to ensure that there is absolute clarity about expectations of both the supervisor and supervisee. They need to decide how best to work together to agreed goals in a way that meets the needs of both – and the needs of the organisation in which they both work. This first conversation, agreeing a contract (or agreement about how the supervision is going to work) is the best opportunity to discuss some of the potential areas of difficulty or anxiety, for example over confidentiality and privacy and the boundaries between supervision and counselling or therapy. It is also the time to acknowledge the fact that there is a power differential between the supervisee and the supervisor and how this will work in the context of the supervision relationship – and opportunity to talk about how the agenda is agreed and how actions are recorded and whether there is any connection to assessments. For example when working with a newly qualified teacher you might want to clearly separate out your "assessment" sessions from sessions that are more about providing support and encouragement. With new supervisees there is likely to be an element of distrust and the more we as supervisors are able to bring that distrust out into the open and discuss it calmly and honestly, the more likely we are to reduce anxiety and build longer term trust for a productive relationship.

8. **It is a time and space for reflection, learning and professional growth.** At its best, supervision is a forum for development for both the supervisor and the supervisee. It is important for the supervisor to go into the session with a genuine sense of enquiry and openness, just as much as

the supervisee. When we learn about good questioning with children, one of the golden rules is to only ask questions that you don't already know the answer to if you want an interesting conversation. The same goes for conversations with your supervisee. If you ask a question that you already know the answer to (or think you do) the supervision session will lose both energy and authenticity as it stumbles into a 'guess what's in my head' game between the supervisee and supervisor, like for example, asking a teacher with some issues around classroom control "is there anything else you should have done before starting the carpet session?". Taking a collaborative approach to reflection and learning can bring amazing insights. For example, a new room leader was discussing the apparent "difficult" behaviour of a team member with her supervisor. The team member was presenting as sullen, uncooperative and disengaged and the new room leader who had tried friendliness and patience was getting desperate – and wondering if she ought to be more directive and possibly think about disciplinary procedures. Able to explore her feelings and thoughts with her supervisor in an open way without feeling judged for her competence, she was able to step back from the day-to-day stress of the situations and explore other options.

Supervision is a time to celebrate the moments of joy, as well as to share concerns

In a collaborative and creative session, the supervisor and supervisee together reached the conclusion that the underlying issue was rooted in a personal fear of being found to be incompetent by the new, more qualified, room leader. All the behaviour was designed to cover up and protect her against being "found out" to be not good enough. The strategy that the supervisor and supervisee came up with was to find opportunities each day to give specific positive feedback to the member of staff about her work in order to build up her confidence and sense of security. In terms of Maslow's hierarchy of need (see Chapter 4) the practitioner was stuck on level two – safety needs. Her anxiety about losing her job was overwhelming her.

9. **It is educative, but does not have a set curriculum.** Unlike some of the processes of induction (see Chapter 4) there are not specific policies and procedures to work through to a particular timetable. In an ongoing supervision relationship, the agenda is best negotiated with both the supervisee and the supervisor bringing issues to discuss as the need arises, although it can also be helpful to have longer term goals that both the supervisor and supervisee are conscious of working towards.

Everyone needs time to think and reflect, particularly in a busy professional life

10. **It is managerial** – in that it relates to organisational standards and policies, but it is not management or appraisal. This is a tricky one. If all supervision conversations are related to a management observation or appraisal then the relationship is unlikely to reach the areas that could result in optimum development. If I think that I am going to be given a mark that could impact on my pay, the security of my job or my staff records I am not likely to risk bringing to the discussion something where I feel I look "bad" or incompetent. I am far more likely to "play it safe", for example, raising the interesting challenge of trying out some of our maths games with the children, rather than risk talking about the day I tried music and movement using my own tape and the children all became wild, uncontrollable goblins and we had to stop the activity rather quickly (that happened to me on my first teaching practice and I was far to embarrassed to bring it up to talk about with my very authoritarian supervisor. We talked about having more visual aids for story time; much safer, but far less interesting or potentially helpful!). However, the likelihood in any supervision model is that there will be a link to appraisal/performance management somewhere – even if only that the same person does both. It is essential to discuss with the supervisee when you are taking on different roles. If supervision is seen as ongoing, then perhaps an annual performance management or appraisal meeting could be clearly signalled as something different, the opportunity to take an overview of strengths and progress, where learning and taking balanced risks are praised.

11. **It is supportive but it is not counselling.** It is vital that supervision is a safe place to explore emotion connected to both work and home, but that it should not be seen as form of counselling or therapy. The supervisor needs to be very secure in her own professionalism to work calmly and constructively, with often strong emotions and also to know when to suggest that a supervisee might find it useful to seek additional professional support.

12. **It is a safe place to express and explore emotion.** Supervisees can be exposed to anxiety, stress and sometimes sadness because of their connection to potentially vulnerable children and their families. They can also meet anger, frustration and resentment in parents who 'blame them' for some incident or are having difficulty managing their own emotions. The supervision relationship is not only an essential 'safety-valve' for the supervisee

to express and examine such feelings objectively, it is also essential for meeting client need. In providing the best support for parents and children we need to be able to listen for both the emotions and the facts in any given situation – both hold valuable pieces of information for our practice. In bringing to a supervision session her concern about the anger expressed by a young mother given the first "book bag" for her child and who "threw her child's book at me shouting she didn't want any of that rubbish in her house!!!" the supervisee and supervisor were able to come up with a number of hypotheses about what might have been the trigger for the angry outburst, without feeling either defensive or vulnerable themselves. The first hypothesis was the right one, the young mother had her own doubts and insecurities about literacy (picked up by the office manager) and the setting was able to sensitively work with the mother until a time came when they were able to support her own learning and development.

Sometimes practitioners may go through periods where they doubt their own competence and the confidence and self-esteem essential for effective practice is placed at risk. Supervision is the safe place to explore those feelings and support the supervisee through this difficult period of uncertainty.

Supervision is a very personal activity, where the relationship between the supervisor and the supervisee is of central importance to the supervision process. It is supportive and challenging. It is open and honest, and recognises the need for accountability. It draws on the strengths of individuals and the organisational context in which they work. That is why the beginning, the time when the supervisor and the supervisee get together to identify how they want to work together, and what they want to work on, is crucial to agreeing a supervision "contract" that will work, and why each contract will be subtly different. Just as each supervisor and supervisee is unique, so is the supervision relationship.

This is important to recognise as what might work for one of your supervisees who loves to talk things through and likes to work things out by sharing them might have to be adjusted for another supervisee who is much more reserved and needs time to think quietly before sharing her thoughts. It is also important as there is no one model of the "perfect" supervisor that you are expected to fit. We work best when we can be authentic. There are, however, some generic characteristics and aptitudes that it is helpful for a supervisor to think about and develop, for example:

Having patience and a sense of humour are important qualities to develop – as a practitioner and as a supervisor

- Being open and honest in dealings with people and in attitude to learning

- Sensitivity to cultural and contextual issues

- The ability to provide challenge and support

- Confidence to manage and support anxiety and other strong emotions

- Patience and a good sense of humour

- Authoritative without being controlling.

Few of us will find all of this easy to take on. Our personal strengths will determine which areas of supervision we are more likely to find comfortable than others. For example, you may find it easier to build up trust and rapport so that your supervisee really opens up to you honestly and thoughtfully, but you find it harder to find the words to give her constructive feedback on areas for development that she has not identified for herself. Alternatively, you may think that one of your strengths is 'telling it like it is' so your supervisees always know exactly where they

Practice example: supervision

What are your supervision strengths? And areas for development?

Tomoko

Tomoko is the manager of a small day nursery and is supervising a new room leader, Toyah. They have been working together for nine months and Toyah has found the supervision relationship hugely supportive and satisfying. She has particularly benefited from the gentle suggestions that Tomoko has made about how to develop different areas of her room and enjoyed it when Tomoko came and worked alongside her. They've also worked well together on planning and observations and supporting individual children in the group with special educational needs.

However, Tomoko knows that some of the parents are not happy with the change in routine in the room, particularly the reduction in time for them to talk to their children's key person and have made some complaints to Tomoko. Tomoko knows she needs to talk about this with Toyah but is worried that she will damage the trusting relationship they have built up.

Sasha

Sasha is a practitioner with three years' experience and is thinking of asking her supervisor about going for promotion.

Her supervisor, Sam, has a very particular style of working with her supervisees. She is very focused on improving the quality of provision in the rooms and is respected by the team because of this. She is also direct, honest and forthright. As Sasha tells her friends: "At least I'm never worried about what Sam is thinking about my work because he just says exactly what he thinks!". This direct feedback has been helpful in drawing attention to Sasha's organisation, which had been a little untidy, and the detail of her planning and display work.

However, the supervision style has also reduced the amount of creativity in her planning, as she is too nervous about making a mistake in front of Sam (who visits the rooms often to check that what is happening matches what is in the planning) to experiment any more.

● What are the supervision strengths for Tomoko and Sam?

What are the areas that it might be helpful for them to develop?

What links do you see to your practice?

stand, but find it harder to listen with patience to the anxieties of a struggling trainee in her first term – when you've already talked about them three times!

Support and challenge

Within the supervision relationship there is an important balance we need to provide in terms of support and challenge so that practitioners are encouraged and supported to become the best they can be, exploring new ideas and skills with confidence and enjoyment. With too much support and too little challenge, the supervision relationship can dwindle into a 'cosy chat' where little learning takes place. With too much challenge and not enough support, the practitioner can become defensive or highly anxious. The place where best supervision – and therefore best learning – takes place is where there is both high challenge and high support, as shown in the table below.

What kind of support and challenge is best for your practitioners and what kind of interventions you need to make in order to provide the best possible opportunity for your supervisees to become outstanding practitioners, will vary according to their level of experience, confidence and learning styles. In the next chapter we look at how you can develop a wide range of different skills and techniques to suit the many different situations you will meet as a supervisor.

What you do also depends on where you are in what we can call the 'supervision cycle'.

Stage one

This is the preparation stage where the supervisor and supervisee meet, build rapport with some general conversation, discuss different items that could be on the agenda for discussion and agree priorities. The role of the supervisor at this point is to be open and curious about what the supervision might bring, reassuring the supervisee of her interest, support and confidentiality.

Stage two

Here the supervisee talks about the event, issue or situation that is the priority. It might be about their concerns over planning or a difficult conversation with a parent. The role of the supervisor at this point is to listen and ask some questions to help clarify the underlying issues for the discussion and therefore the goal. For example, a supervisee may arrive at a meeting saying that

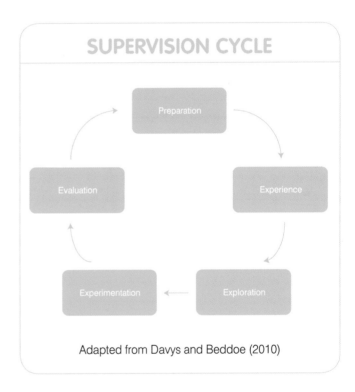

SUPERVISION CYCLE

Preparation

Experience

Exploration

Experimentation

Evaluation

Adapted from Davys and Beddoe (2010)

Balancing support and challenge

High challenge	Practitioners feel under pressure, can lose confidence or become defensive and avoid taking risks – preferring to "play it safe".	Practitioners explore new ideas with confidence and enjoyment, trying new skills and reflecting honestly on their strengths and areas for development.
Low challenge	An unhappy, dispiriting place to work where standards tend to drift downwards.	Practitioners tend to carry on with what they are doing, and can become complacent or a little bored.
	Low support	**High support**

she feels overwhelmed with her planning and assessment and doesn't feel she can manage. It is the role of the supervisor to help get underneath the general to the specific – is the issue time management or knowledge about child development? Is it lack of confidence that is holding her back or does she need some support with her organisation of files and information?

Stage three

This is where the supervisor encourages the supervisee to go a bit more deeply into the issue, reflecting back, summarising and helping the supervisee reflect on and express her feelings and behaviours in a more objective way. Our supervisee, with the anxiety about planning and assessment, might have identified a combination of lack of organisation skill and experience and at the same time a lack of confidence in what the content is. The supervisor's role is to listen, explore and clarify. The temptation is to leap in here with the solution, but this can encourage dependency and deepen the lack of confidence. It is usually much more effective for the supervisee to come up with her own solutions, or to work collaboratively to identify some possible approaches to try out in Stage four. It is sometimes enjoyable and energising to end in a brainstorm where both supervisee and supervisor spend 10 minutes thinking of lots of options and possibilities without analysing how good they are, before sitting down and deciding what option look best.

Stage four

In Stage four the supervisee and the supervisee agree on what actions to take from the options generated, what support and

resources might be needed and timescales for implementation. For example, in our example the supervisee may decide to do some joint planning with her colleague in on Thursday afternoons and to focus on two children a week for assessments to bring to her next supervision. The supervisor agrees to talk to the room leader and broker the arrangement, and to be available at 8.00am on Fridays for the supervisee to bring any questions about planning or assessment so these don't build up over time. She also agrees to pay for a relevant CPD course next month.

Stage five

As part of the ongoing supervision (remember effective supervision isn't just about what happens in a single meeting but is part of the day-to-day relationship in the setting), the supervisor helps the supervisee to evaluate the impact of what she is doing, how it is helping to both improve the quality of her assessments and planning and build up her confidence.

The outcomes from the supervision in terms of evaluation are also brought to the next supervision session to feed into the next round of issues, exploration and experimentation.

For each of these stages there are specific skills that can help the supervisor provide focused support and challenge. These range from the most directive (e.g. telling the supervisee where to find the information she needs to plan an outing) to the least directive (listening with genuine curiosity to learn more about the supervisee and his or her issue). In between, there is a whole range of different interventions to have in your toolbox. We will explore these in the next chapter.

KEY POINTS IN AN INTRODUCTION TO SUPERVISION

In this chapter we have looked at the purpose and value of supervision, the supervision cycle and the skills and attributes that support the most effective supervision practice and how to provide a balance of support and challenge. If you already have supervision in your setting, think about how it works for you and for the supervisee.

- How clear are you about your role? How clear is the supervisee?

- How do you ensure a good balance of challenge and support?

- How do you ensure that you get to talk about the really important things?

- How comfortable are you with managing emotions?

- What are your strengths as a supervisor? What areas might you want to develop further?

Chapter 6

Coaching skills for supervision

"A coach is a person who helps me to think through how to get from where I am to where I need or want to be"
Joy and Pask (2011).

I have called this chapter 'coaching skills for supervision' because I want to emphasise the benefit of using a reflective learning, or coaching, model of supervision. However, all these skills can be used in many other situations, for example by a mentor with a mentee, with a student coordinator and a student, or by interested practitioners supporting and challenging each other through peer coaching.

The table below is taken and adapted from some work by the School of Coaching. It shows the wide range of interventions open to supervisors providing support and challenge to their supervisees.

For example, for practitioners new to the setting or new to the profession there is going to be a lot of information that they simply have to be 'told'. An induction handbook can be a very useful way of working through essential information systematically, perhaps with a mentor who can also provide essential practical advice in the early days of a career.

Modelling is a very powerful way to share practical skills and techniques, for example talking with children or telling a story, encouraging experimentation and problem solving or supporting active learning.

NON-DIRECTIVE

PUSH
Solving someone's problem for them

Listening to understand

Reflecting back

Paraphrasing

Asking questions that raise awareness

Making suggestions

Modelling

Offering feedback

PULL
Helping someone solve their own problems

Giving advice

Telling

DIRECTIVE

From the School of Coaching

If you are using modelling to support staff development it is imperative that you explain what you are doing and why; provide opportunity for discussion and learning, otherwise your new practitioner may simply note what a good storyteller you are without making the connections you are assuming she will make to her own practice. I have put modelling on the continuum diagram to the left as it was not in the initial School of Coaching list – but has much to offer the early years setting as a development tool.

Giving advice and making suggestions

Giving advice has to be used cautiously. It can cause defensiveness when we offer it without being asked, for example, how often have you given advice to a member of staff, for them to say: "I've tried that already" or "that wouldn't work here"? Alternatively, if a supervisee comes to you regularly for advice, it can encourage dependency. You don't want to develop a supervision relationship where you are seen as the font of all wisdom and your supervisee approaches you for advice about every part of the day. On the other hand, you do want to be helpful and constructive in developing effective practice.

To develop confidence we would probably want to start with using open questions to encourage our supervisees to think more deeply about the issue/problem and maybe come up their own solutions. However there are two occasions when we might want to give information or suggestions:

- If there is important information that we have and our supervisee does not, for example about health and safety or patterns of child development. If that is the case we should just tell the supervisee what he/she needs to know.

- If you've tried open questions to encourage reflections and you feel that the supervisee is really stuck, then presenting your ideas as a suggestion rather than advice can be a better option as it still leaves the supervisee the responsibility of deciding how to act on the advice, as in the following example.

Supervisee: I'm worried about Mary in my group; that she's not settling into nursery well. Can you give me some advice?

Supervisor: Tell me a little more about what it is that's making you anxious.

Supervisee: She always seems to be on her own and she's very quiet and I'm worried that she might be not enjoying nursery as much as she might be.

Supervisor: What have you already tried?

Supervisee: I've tried to involve her in other children's games sometimes but she doesn't seem interested. I'm not sure what to do next.

Supervisor: I'm not going to give you advice here because you are the one in the room who knows what's going on and so you are the expert here! But would it be helpful if I made a couple of suggestions for you to think about?

Supervisee: Yes please!

Supervisor: If you've not already tried it, you might like to try playing alongside her yourself for some slightly longer periods than you usually do. That could help you find out a bit more about what she's thinking and feeling. And if you think she might like to play with some other children but isn't sure how to go about it, you might model that for her a bit, for example if you're playing in the home corner you might say to Mary: "Oh look, there's Tajin. I wonder if she'd like some ice-cream too. Tajin, we're having a party, would you like to come and have some ice-cream?". On the other hand, she might be happy with her own thoughts and play and having other children at that stage might feel like a distraction for her – you'd have to judge.

Supervisee: Thank you. I like the playing with her idea. I can see how it could give me a better idea of what is going on for her.

Listening

As early years practitioners, we tend to be excellent at finding the time to sit and listen to children, but in a busy setting it can be difficult sometimes to find the time and space to really listen to our practitioners. When we do find the time, the gains for the practitioner, for the setting and for you as a manager can be enormous.

Tasha had recently become the room leader for the three to four-year-olds and was finding it very hard going. The other two members of staff had been working in the setting for a long time and it seemed that everything she suggested had already been

What are your strengths as a listener?

When I am listening to someone talking, I:	Usually = 2 marks	Sometimes = 1 mark
Listen carefully to what the speaker is saying without judging them		
Stop myself from finishing sentences, even when there are pauses in the conversation whilst the speaker is thinking		
Let them finish without interrupting to make my own point		
Look at the person who is talking, noticing significant body language		
Listen for the feelings and the facts		
Control fidgeting or doodling		
Only ask questions that help me to understand more about what the speaker is trying to say, or encouraging them to continue		
Often repeat what they say in my own words to check that I've understood		
Stop myself from planning what I'm going to say when they've finished		
Can tune-out other thoughts or demands, even when I'm busy		
Am conscious of my own body language, and use it to signal that I'm listening		
Score		

done or was impossible "with these children". Staff meetings were becoming more and more negative and Mary was feeling stuck and rather isolated, as conversations during breaks were tense. During one of her performance management meetings, her line manager asked her some questions that gave her a new insight into the problem. First she asked her: "If the problem was sorted, what would be happening?" and Tasha realised that it felt more important to her now to be feeling that they were a team working together than for her to get going on her ideas for changing the room routines. The second question was: "What's stopping that from happening" and Tasha answered quite simply that she didn't know. In her enthusiasm for the new job and anxiety to prove that she could be a room leader, she realised that nearly all the conversations had centred round what her plans were, and she didn't know what the practitioners were thinking, apart from their negative response to her suggestions. Her line manager suggested that she spent some time talking, and more importantly, listening to the practitioners

to find out more about them, their interests, strengths and anxieties – and what mattered to them.

Tajin set aside 20 minutes the next week to spend time with each of the practitioners. She explained that it wasn't a line management meeting; it was an opportunity to talk to them properly about their work and get to know them a bit better. She made coffee and bought some fruit and cakes and sat down to listen. She learned about their careers to date, their families, their hobbies and where they were going on holiday. She also learned that they had had a room leader a few years ago who changed everything very quickly and all the children got upset and confused. The parents complained and there was a lot of unpleasantness. What was more, all the changes happened suddenly and without being discussed with the practitioners and they felt they never knew what was happening next. Tasha realised that it was change they were anxious about, rather than the specifics of Tasha's suggestions. She went back to her manager (who hadn't been at the setting when the difficulties had occurred) and together they thought up a strategy to build up the confidence of the practitioners and introduce any changes slowly, steadily and with lots of consultation and preparation time. It worked.

Taking the time to listen to your staff may not reveal anything quite so crucial as Tasha discovered, but there are lots of other things to find out that don't tend to be revealed during casual chats in the staff room. When people are really listened to, you tend to find out what is really important to them at that time, what their values are and what is motivating them – or not motivating them.

Listening for real meaning is not as easy as it sounds. There is an art to it. The next time you have a conversation with someone about something important to them, try listening at these three different levels:

1. What are the facts? Facts are important. Is it every parent that has complained about the letter that went out last night? Or just four?

2. What are the feelings? The practitioner may always let you know their feelings directly but the careful listener will be able to spot them. Sometimes someone presents as angry, but a bit more listening reveals that she is more anxious and afraid. Look out for body language as well as listening to the tone of voice and the words used. If someone says she is "devastated" by what a parent said, that's an important word. You might want to ask her if she'd like to tell you more about what devastated means to her.

3. Listen for the values, what matters to the practitioner – that is likely to give you the best clues into what the conversation is really about. For example, in a conversation with Tasha, a, new practitioner, she kept going back to examples of the children's creativity, used creative language and images and examples. What she was ostensibly talking about was her frustration with the planning system. Careful listening was

helpful here in identifying both the cause of the problem and a possible route through. Initially Tasha had said that the problem was that the paperwork for planning was just too much of a burden and she didn't have time for it. It became clear that the real problem was that she felt that the planning system constrained both her creativity and the children's. Knowing that, the task of helping her see her way to using the planning system constructively became much clearer. We looked at examples of creativity that she'd thought about supporting or introducing to the children and discussed how the planning system could accommodate that.

If you scored between 16 and 22, you already have many active listening skills. Most of us have areas that we need to work on throughout our lives in order to make best use of our time communicating with others. Use your learning journal to jot down some ideas for how you could improve your active listening skills.

Questioning

Just as we find when working with children, the most powerful questions tend to be open, not closed. In a typical coaching conversation you will probably ask four different kinds of questions:

1. Questions to help establish what are the most important issues to talk about (Goals)

2. Questions to check out what the reality of the situation really is, what's really going on (Reality)

3. Questions to help identify different things that could be done to help make progress towards the goal (Options) and

4. Questions that support practitioners in clarifying what actions they might take (Will).

As you practise with your team you will build up your own bank of useful questions, but the table on the right gives you some ideas to start you off.

Do not be tempted to work through these questions as a list – it will exhaust both of you! Knowing what is the most useful question to ask will come with practise, and more importantly from really listening to your client and genuinely wanting to know the answers to the questions you choose. Sometimes the best question is just a pause after a response with "mmmm?" or repeating a particularly important word, or a generalisation

POINT FOR REFLECTION

Never underestimate the power of good listening. If you can think of a time when someone has really listened to you when it mattered you will remember how powerful it can be.

Useful questions for a coaching conversation

Goals	Reality
What would you like us to think about today?	Does that happen all the time, or just sometimes?
How've you got on since we last met?	What would happen if you do nothing about this?
What's going really well for you at the moment?	What is your own responsibility for what is happening?
What isn't going quite so well?	Who owns this problem?
Is there anything else that is important for you at the moment that we haven't talked about?	How important is it that something happens here?
What would be most useful for us to work on together today?	How often does X happen? Always? Sometimes? When?
What makes this/these things important now?	What have you already tried?
What would a successful session today look like for you?	What early signs are there that things are getting better?
How can I best help you with this issue/these problems?	What is standing in the way of you achieving your goals/dreams?
What will be different if you achieve your goal? What will you be thinking? feeling? doing?	What might you have to give up in order to achieve your goal?
Tell me more about…?	What energy/skills can you bring to the situation?
Can I summarise what we've discussed so far? (this works well in each stage of the conversation)	What resources have you got to help you?
So what is the crux of the matter…?	
How important is that/are those issues for you on a scale of 1-10?	

Options	Will
What has worked in similar situations?	What's your first/next step?
What might your best friend advise you?	When are you going to take it?
What would you advise yourself – at your most resourceful?	Who can help you?
What might you advise a friend struggling with a similar situation?	How will you know you are making progress against your goals?
What is your ideal solution?	
If you could wave a magic wand, what would you like to happen?	
What criteria are you going to use to judge which option to go with?	
What option seems the best one?	
What other options do you have?	

that you'd like to check. For example in this conversation with Molly, Elsie reflecting back the word "never" opened up a different way of thinking for Molly.

Elsie: What would you like us to think about today?

Molly: Ethan's behaviour! It's just getting worse and worse and nothing I do seems to make any difference!! He never settles to anything.

Elsie: Never?

Molly: (Pause) Well I suppose that he's calmer when we go outside and he's often happy for a while in the sandpit.

Elsie: Tell me more about what is happening in the sand pit…

Molly: Mmmm (thinking) He likes it best when he's got lots of room and usually sits for a while just running sand through his fingers… and then he sometimes likes to fill up different containers and pour them out too…

Elsie: (summarising) so when he's in the sandpit his behaviour is calmer and he becomes engaged in different pouring activities?

Molly: Yessss (thinking and smiling a bit).

Elsie: Are there any other time when he seems calmer and/or more engaged?

Molly: Maybe in the water tray…and that's pouring things too! And he also likes squeezing new play dough.

Elsie: So if you were advising your best friend on how to support Ethan in the nursery, what do you think you might suggest?

Molly: I'd suggest that she looked for more opportunities for him to do pouring activities and to enjoy feeling different textures in his hands…

Elsie: Is there anything else you might do?

Molly: (Pause) …and maybe spend more time with him when he's enjoying those times rather than thinking 'Phew, a few minutes peace' (laughs!).

Elsie: So, what's your first step going to be?

Using a coaching approach can help to increase everyone's confidence

Molly: I'm going to go and have a look at my planning for tomorrow and see what we've got that is going to appeal to Ethan, and I'm going to make sure that I have time to spend with him calmly joining in his favourite play.

One of the most difficult parts of the session can be getting started on something that feels purposeful and active.

Your role during the 'goals' part of the session might be to frequently reflect back to your supervisee what you are hearing, for example:

> "So can I just check with you that I'm getting all the important points? I think that you were saying that you're pleased with the way your planning is going, that you are enjoying your time in the baby room more, but that you are still feeling very anxious about talking to parents and a bit nervous about the parents' evening coming up?".

It is helpful to give this kind of summarising with a gentle questioning tone so that your supervisee will feel fine about coming in and saying: "Actually it's not that, it's something else…". If that happens, don't worry that you "got it wrong".

It is good news as it shows that your summarising is helping your supervisee clarify and express thoughts more strongly. Having summarised, it might be helpful to then ask a direct question about goals, such as:

"What might be a useful goal for us to have?"

The practitioner might then suggest something like…

"To be more confident about going and talking to the parents when they arrive in the mornings and to know what would be good things to say at the meeting".

Sometimes you might (especially at the beginning of the relationship) have to ask some more goal questions like:

"So, thinking about your work with parents, what would a successful session today look like? What would you like to go away with?".

If the supervisee remains 'stuck' you could tentatively suggest some possible options based on her responses to date, for example:

"Correct me if I'm wrong, but is the goal we're focusing on here about you feeling more confident with talking to parents when they drop off and pick up their children?".

Feedback

Listening to your staff is an excellent tool for encouraging self-reflection and building up resourcefulness. However, that does not mean that we should ever shirk giving honest feedback. If we do not tell our practitioners what needs to change, they are not going to know they need to change.

Feedback is probably one of the most powerful tools in the manager's tool-box. But it is also a very tricky one to get right and worth spending some time thinking about.

At its best, feedback is motivating, energising and empowering. If we don't give honest feedback to our staff we are letting them down because how can they change and grow if they do not know what they should be doing differently?

However, feedback done badly can be cripplingly destructive. In this section we will look at what makes for successful feedback and how to avoid it becoming demotivating.

One of the most motivating pieces of incidental feedback that I have had recently, came from a student I was working with in a nursery school. She was struggling to find her natural, authoritative style with the children. She was great at listening to them and supporting their thinking in small groups. But when it came to getting their attention when there were other things they wanted to do she couldn't seem to find her natural authority.

Usually the role of the tutor is a fairly quiet one, tucked away in a corner with a file or two. But on this occasion I decided a different approach was needed. We put the files aside and did some role play, trying out different approaches on each other and then with the children. It was energising and fun and at the end of it the student had 'found' her voice.

The feedback she gave me was: "I know this sounds stupid, but I hadn't realised what a good teacher you were. That was a really useful session". And that feedback changed my practice as a tutor. I realised that actually I am a teacher, and that meant doing things, not just looking at files and talking. From then on I took a much more active approach to my work with students – and enjoyed it much more too.

On the other hand, an example of cripplingly demotivating feedback was given to me when I was 13. I can still remember it vividly. I had a school report that said in P. E. (Physical Education) "Jane lacks ability, effort and enthusiasm." Well, it was true that I certainly didn't have a talent in that area and that I was trying to cover up my embarrassment about my poor hand/eye coordination with a bit of a laugh and a joke now and then, but that feedback did not make me increase my efforts. Instead I simply gave up on all kinds of organised sport for over 20 years!

If we think of the core purpose of feedback being to change practitioner behaviour then we need to make sure that it does that job – and does not demotivate.

The key to getting feedback right is to understand the difference between feedback and criticism.

In your learning journal write a list of words that describe **feedback**. Then write a list that describes **criticism**. When you have finished compare your list with table on page 50.

Sometimes it's easier to decide what we want to say than to find the actual words to say it. The feedback list can be a helpful way of finding the right words.

Describing feedback table

Feedback	Criticism
Where possible, builds on a strength	Always focuses on the negative
Looks to the future	Concentrates on what happened in the past
Solution-focused	Looks for someone to blame
About facts	Often generalises
Says "and"	Says "but"
Is two-way	Is one-way

LINKS WITH YOUR PRACTICE

Using the feedback column as a guide, think about how you could give feedback to these practitioners in the following scenarios.

How could you help to change their behaviour and motivate them to work towards achieving their full potential?

- You've just taken over from an outstanding room leader. Everyone is very confident and clear about what they do and how, but you would like them to tune-in a bit more to the children's play, have a bit more reflection time for adults **and** children.

- Your strongest practitioner has asked for feedback as she's thinking about promotion. She's very proud of her observations and wants to start with these. You've noticed that they are long and not always to the point…

- Your new team member is regularly late. She always has an excuse as she comes through the door…

- Your weak student doesn't seem to be making much progress in her planning. She's keen and willing and has a sensitive way of talking to the children but her file is almost empty and her ideas for focus experiences for the children are usually rather dull (although she always says that she's following the children's ideas).

For example: Jane is an experienced member of staff with a particular way of putting up displays. They are neat and attractive. You'd like them to be more interactive and child-centred. What feedback are you going to give her?

Feedback – Possible things to say

Where possible, builds on a strength: Thank you for putting up that new display in the entrance hall about the work we've been doing on children's speaking and listening. Your displays are always beautifully presented and show how you value the children's work.

Solution-focused: I'd like us to build on that to include more ideas from the children about how to display their work, perhaps with some captions using their own words.

Looks to the future: So, when we do the next display can we get together first and think of some more ideas about how this might work?

POINT FOR REFLECTION

Think of a time when you have received feedback that has been motivating.

Now think of a time when you have been given feedback that has demotivated you.

What did the person giving the feedback say or do? What did you feel? What did you say or do?

POINT FOR REFLECTION

People often forget the things that were said, they never forget how you made them feel. Getting feedback right is important.

About facts: Most of our displays at the moment look beautiful and I know the parents enjoy them, **and** I think that if we just made a couple of changes they'd be a really useful resource to help with the children's learning too.

Is two-way: On a slightly different issue, I've been trying to put up some information for parents **and** I just can't get it organised to it looks attractive and engage the interest of the parents. Could you give me some feedback on how to do that differently?

Says… "and" not "but": The way you've displayed the work we've been doing on speaking **and** listening is very attractive and I'd like us to now bring some of the children's thoughts and ideas into the display to make it even more interactive – can you think of some ideas to help us to do that?

Think about how much more motivating that is than…

"The way you've displayed the work we've been doing on speaking and listening is very attractive **but**…" When we hear the word "but" we nearly always feel a sinking feeling that stops us listening to what has gone well and just focuses on what we've done "wrong".

How do you make sure that your feedback is purposeful and motivating?

KEY POINTS IN COACHING SKILLS FOR SUPERVISION

In this chapter we have worked through some key supervision skills that you can use to help your members of staff develop in competence and confidence.

Think about the different practitioners you are supporting in your setting. What opportunities do you have to listen regularly to them and give honest and motivating feedback on their work?

● What questions do you use most in order to help your practitioners reflect on their practice and start to build their own solutions?

| What are your strengths as a coach for your team?

| What might be your areas for development?

Chapter 7

Change and action planning

"What size do you want to be" the caterpillar asked Alice. "Oh, I'm not particular as to size, only one doesn't like changing quite so often you know" she replied.
From *Alice in Wonderland* by Lewis Carroll.

Change can be exciting, invigorating and rewarding. It is also a highly complex and often stressful process, even when it's something we are reasonably comfortable with or looking forward to. We are unlikely to find ourselves suddenly growing to be as tall as a house and then shrinking to mouse-size as Alice did in Wonderland, but we may often find ourselves having to change our planning or assessments, our routines, our curriculum, the people we work with, our timetables and

How do you feel about change?

our environment. As leaders we also have to support our teams through changes too.

"Leadership for change requires vision and inspiration, careful planning, decision making skills, effective communication, confident conflict management and sensitive handling of people involved or affected by the change" Jillian Rodd, *Leadership in Early Childhood*.

Change is probably the one constant in our professional lives. At the time of writing we are adjusting to a revised EYFS framework and responding to the demands of a revised Ofsted. There are also changes in the system to fund two-year-olds and huge changes in the way local authorities are providing support and challenge to schools and the private and voluntary sector. Supporting our staff through change so that they feel confident, competent and energised requires us to understand the change process itself.

In the preceding chapters we have seen how understanding about motivation, coaching and mentoring can enable us to show practitioners that we value their work and also to provide appropriate support for their ongoing development. In Chapter 3 we looked at the importance of vision, being clear in our own minds where the better future lies, what we want in the long term for our children and their families and how we can involve our teams in sharing that vision. This chapter looks in more detail about motivation in terms of managing the process of change, and how action planning can provide a practical framework for teams to work together to achieve the outcomes associated with your vision for the setting. The following chapter will address issues around possible problems that may arise in leadership, including conflict management.

Motivators

Essentially there are two great motivators for change. The first is the need to address something that isn't going well, for example being told by Ofsted that your planning does not adequately support the needs of different groups of children in your setting – boys or children with special educational needs for example. The second is to perceive something that might provide more benefits than the *status quo*, for example, a new leader who casts a fresh eye over the available space and sees how it might be possible to create room for a larger messy area so that the creativity of both practitioners and children can have more opportunity to do really big pieces of 3D art and design.

Psychologists tell us that changing because we realise we have a problem can be a very efficient catalyst, but that seeing a solution that will bring significant benefits is what will generate the greater energy. So, if you are working with your team on improving your model for planning then, pointing out that if you continue with the way you are going will bring trouble when Ofsted calls, might just catch people's attention and increase their focus on the discussion you are leading. On the other hand, if you quickly move on to the benefits of the change – reduced paperwork, children making more progress, parents more satisfied, headteacher or owner delighted, Ofsted impressed – then you will tend to find that your team will start to find the creative, emotional and physical energy to join with you in moving towards a "better future".

One of the ways we can tune-in to the complexity of managing change is by thinking about the work we do with children supporting them through transitions. We know, for example, that there are things we can do to support our children if they are moving to a new setting or a new phase in their education that include helping children see the positives in the change, giving them time to acknowledge the feelings that come from leaving a familiar and trusted environment (including the people) and supporting them to develop their knowledge and skills so that they can make the transition with pride and confidence.

This process mirrors very closely the model William Bridges (1991) gives us to help understand the change process in general. He believes that the reason we can find change difficult is not so much to do with the practical things that are happening as the underlying psychological issues that we are dealing with as part of our 'transition'.

William Bridges' theory is that when we experience a transition, we move through three different phases and if we better understand these phases then we can provide improved support for ourselves and our teams in the management of change. He called the three phases: **Ending, Losing, and Letting Go**, **The Neutral Zone** and **The New Beginning**, and whilst the phases

Transitions can be exciting, but need to be planned for

do roughly happen in that order, there is always going to be a certain amount of fluidity between them too.

Using William Bridges' theory to help manage change in a nursery class

For nearly fifty years, the nursery at Holly Bush Primary had been in a small building separate from the main Infants' School. In 1996 it had expanded to become a larger setting with a mixture of full and part-time places to the equivalent of 39 full-time places. The expansion had been achieved by knocking down storage and the staff room to create a larger central space. Since then, the head, the governors and the nursery staff had all been campaigning to get a new nursery building that would be less cramped and offer more space for parents, small groups etc. In 2010 they got lucky. A new building was commissioned that would be fit for purpose and join to the main infant building – which would support more collaboration and partnership working with the Reception class and other colleagues such as the IT coordinator and the new library. Initially there were many

Keeping everyone informed is an important part of managing change successfully

Being able to talk about what we would miss and also identify what we would be taking with us – just because the kitchen was going didn't mean that we wouldn't have other times together in a different space (*clarifying what would change and what would stay the same*)

Keeping everybody informed about what was happening, and getting involved in some of the decision making – for example the design of the new parents room and the doors from the indoor to the outdoor area (*ensuring excellent communications and involving everyone in the practicalities*)

Planning and hosting a grand old-nursery party for the children and parents – and we also invited old members of staff along (*acknowledging and celebrating the ending, whatever it is*)."

(2) **The Neutral Zone** – this can be roughly summed up as the time when the ending has sort of happened, but the beginning hasn't really begun, although there will be aspects of endings and beginnings happening at the same time. Typically people can find this a difficult stage, when everything feels uncertain and confused, where energy dips and depression can sneak in when we're not looking. As a leader this is where you can help your team by encouraging new thinking and exploration, as well as providing a calm and supportive backdrop.

"The neutral zone kicked in right after the party. We hadn't been able to have it on the last day of term because of timetables so there was another month to go. It felt flat coming in the day after the party. There seemed nothing to plan for. We'd done all the packing we could before the children left. The building was nearly completed and the packers booked to come in towards the end of the holiday to help us move. Some members of the team got summer colds – which I knew was a symptom of us all being a bit under par.

Having a conversation with the headteacher helped me get some perspective on what was happening and start to see how we could use this time productively. She was very understanding about what a difficult time it was, and how we should make sure we were extra kind to each other as everybody would be feeling a bit 'wobbly', but she also gave me ideas about things we could do to start prepare for the new nursery, even though we weren't in it yet:

We used our staff meetings to focus on what would be happening next term, thinking about new routines we

celebrations and a great deal of excitement about the architect's drawings. Then came the time to pack up and move and the nursery head, Cynthia, was finding it hard going…

(1) **Ending, Losing, and Letting Go** – helping people deal with feelings of loss and mentally let go and prepare to move on.

"As we started to pack things away I noticed that practitioners were starting to get irritable with each other and the work seemed to get slower and slower. Using the William Bridges model I encouraged people to talk about what they were feeling and it brought out so many different things. Everyone was really keen on the new building, but they were worrying about not having so much autonomy when we were part of the "big school" and were anxious about the new space not working so well for team teaching. There was also a nostalgia creeping in about the old kitchen and all the chats we'd had huddled together talking about the children, planning and problem solving.

I realised that just like some children moving to "big school" we were having some issues about leaving our old nursery building. What helped us move on was actually verbalising our feelings and talking about how to manage them, including:

could try out and ordering new resources to make the most of the increased space.
(*Focusing on the future.*)

- We also spent some time reflecting on what we had learned about working together both in the old nursery and in preparing for the new – what being a good team meant to us and how we could build on this to support each other in the new building whilst also getting to know the other staff better.
(*Encouraging learning from reflection, taking time to think.*)

- The other thing that really helped was the timing of the move. We had the summer holidays to get used to the fact that we were not going to be coming back to the old building and start to feel excited about the new building.
(*Building in a real "neutral" zone to provide real time and space between significant endings and new beginnings, maybe a holiday, or a weekend – that is why it often seems to work better with new planning or new routines to start after a natural break.*)"

(3) **The New Beginning** – the role of the leader here is to help practitioners get in touch with their positive energy for the new beginning, help them feel a real sense of purpose and come to terms with their new role. This rarely happens on the first day of the new beginning; people take time to psychologically make the transition.

> "*It is normal to feel doubts about competence and capability at this stage. It is also normal for there to be a dip in confidence a few weeks in when the reality of the new situation begins to become clear.*" Jenny Rogers, Coaching Skills.

"The new nursery looked stunning. The colours were just what we'd hoped for and the outdoor area looked so different from the pile of mud we'd left behind. Everybody was really pleased, but I could tell that people were feeling a bit nervous too, for example we were much more visible now than we had been and the head popped in far more frequently. She was being very supportive but I could tell that some practitioners were feeling a bit self-conscious. There were moments of confusion too when people couldn't find stuff and there was a bit of anxiety around in the mornings as everything seemed to take so long.

What helped us through this stage were:

- Taking time to talk about what had gone well at the end of each day, reminding ourselves of our strengths, and using this to explore things we might want to do differently. I

was careful to emphasise building on our strengths, not to talk about "weaknesses" as I thought that might add to feelings of insecurity.
(*Focus on what successful looks like, look for 'quick wins'.*)

- Making sure that communication was spot on – that everybody knew what was happening, and involving the team in decisions as they came up, like how to set up outside in the mornings now the parents were also gathering there after dropping off older children
(*The more we are involved with change the less scary it is, nobody enjoys change that is 'done to' them.*)

- Using the opportunity of our first parents' coffee morning to have a bit of a "house warming", inviting the head and a couple of other members of staff from the main school and some governors. It really helped to talk to everyone about the advantages of our new building – made it seem more real to us.
(*Symbolic parties or other kinds of events help us to psychologically acknowledge and come to terms with change – both endings and beginnings.*)"

Three lessons from the world of psychology

The essence of good leadership is essentially about making sure that your team feels good about what they are doing **now** whilst also providing them with a picture of a **better future** that they can relate to, engage with and where they can focus their efforts productively. To do these both at the same time requires all the skills above plus a highly developed emotional intelligence:

- **Understanding yourself:** your goals, intentions, responses, behaviour and feelings, and

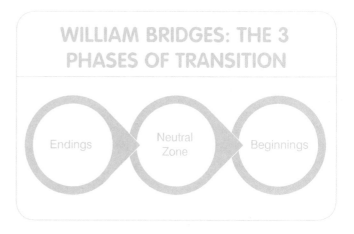

WILLIAM BRIDGES: THE 3 PHASES OF TRANSITION

Endings   Neutral Zone   Beginnings

Understanding others: their goals, intentions, responses, behaviours and feelings.

In their book *Yes! 50 secrets from the science of Persuasion*, Goldstein, Martin and Cialdini share with us 50 different social influence strategies drawn from a wider variety of psychological research. I've called this section lessons from the world of psychology and it is important to emphasise, as the authors do, that this is not about manipulating people. It's about using our emotional intelligence, informed by knowledge of what motivates others, how their values impact on behaviour and what different responses might mean.

I've chosen three examples that resonate for me with our work.

Lesson one:
Start with small steps

"*A journey of a thousand miles begins with a single step*"
The Way of Lao-tzu, Lao-tzu, Chinese philosopher.

The research quoted in *YES!* tells us about a road safety initiative in a wealthy neighbourhood. Residents were asked to display a sign in their gardens that said 'Drive Carefully'. Only 17% agreed. In another, similar district a different researcher initially approached residents with a small card to display in their window saying, 'Be a Safe Driver'. Because it was a small request, nearly everyone agreed. Two weeks later when the researcher returned with the larger request about a sign in the garden, a surprising 76% agreed. The psychology, we are told, is that:

POINT FOR REFLECTION

Think about some of the big changes you have made in your career. What did you do that helped you make the change? What hindered or was less helpful? What did other people do or say that was helpful or less helpful?

Now think about someone else you have helped or supported through a change. What do you think you did that was most helpful? Less helpful?

How might making a small step first have helped?

"*Having agreed to the initial request, the residents came to see themselves as committed to worthy causes such as safe driving. When these home owners were approached a couple of weeks later, they were motivated to act consistently with this perception of themselves as concerned citizens*" Goldstein et al.

How does this help us in our work in the early years? As leaders we may sometimes see something that needs to be done that is quite a big change for many practitioners. If we can find a small step that practitioners feel safe and secure with, this can help change their motivation towards the bigger change further down the line.

For example, if you want to introduce free-flow, you might suggest doing it one day a week for a trial period. Or if you want to introduce differentiated planning for different groups of children, you may choose to start with one group, which you know your team is particularly interested in or concerned about: "let's focus this week on children with speech and language delay – see what we might do a bit differently in the role play area to support their development".

One small step in the right direction is a good start...

Lesson two: The waiter's tip

Can you guess which waiters get the biggest tips? Those who smile? Chat to you? Arrive quickly?

None of those – the waiters who get the biggest tips are those who accurately reflect back to the customers what the customers have just ordered. For example, if I ask for:

"Two roast chickens, a mixed salad a jug of water"

The research says that my tip is likely to be nearly 70% higher if the waiter responds with:

"So, you'd like two roast chickens, a mixed salad and a jug of water." Rather than:

"OK", "Yes" or even "two chickens, salad and water".

For maximum response you need exactly the same words in the same order. This makes perfect sense when you think how irritating it can be when you are trying to explain something to someone and they keep getting the really important word wrong. I was a volunteer "client" once for an end of course assessment. The trainee coaches had to coach me on something I had identified whilst their tutors observed and made an assessment on their coaching practice. I had a very warm and personable young woman working with me and in general the session was going well, until I got to the part where I was explaining my dilemma over a new job which was a bit like an advisor's job. She kept using the word 'inspector' instead of 'advisor', even though I explained that it was not an inspector role. Because I felt that she didn't understand the importance of the word advisor I could not tune-in to the other things she was saying.

When we are helping our colleagues manage a particularly difficult change there may be times when they come to talk to you to explain their concerns, anxieties or reservations. What the "waiter's tip" teaches us is the value of really tuning-in to what they are saying and showing that we've heard and understood exactly what they are saying. Look at the following example where the foundation stage leader uses the teacher's own words to diffuse the initial confrontation and then lead into explaining her reasons for making what had been an unpopular decision.

Teacher: I feel really upset that you've asked Simone to organise the parents evening this term. I've always done it in the past and I've had really good feedback too.

Foundation Stage Leader: I know you've done it before and that you've had really good feedback and I can understand completely why you are feeling upset. In fact I should have thought of this earlier and explained my reasons before I talked to Simone. I'm sorry. The reason I wanted Simone to do it as it is an important part of her professional development to have the opportunity to organise a meeting with parents, and it's something she just hasn't done. On the other hand, I know it's something that you're really good at and I was going to ask you if you'd be able to organise the open day for new parents a bit later this term as it's a more complicated event and I think you've got the right experience.

Teacher: Thank you. That makes much more sense now and I'd be really interested in taking on the new parents' meeting.

Goldstein et al. argue convincingly that the reason behind this is the "mirroring" effect – that when one person mirrors another's behaviour either verbally or non-verbally, it builds trust and helps to create a kind of "bond" or rapport. Using the right words shows you have really listened (like the waiters!) and can therefore be more trusted with the matter in hand. If the foundation stage leader had used "angry" or "irritated" instead of "upset" then it would almost certainly have distracted the teacher from listening further to what the leader had to say. She would have probably felt the need to reiterate that she was "upset" until she felt that word had been heard, and it might have meant that she was less receptive to hearing the "reasons" and may have taken longer to agree to take on the new parents' meeting as she was still stuck in being upset.

LINKS WITH YOUR PRACTICE

Next time you are talking to someone about something important, notice their body language. Look at how she or he is sitting, where their arms are, what they are doing with their hands, their legs. How straight is their back? What is their expression like – are they smiling or frowning?

Sometimes just noticing what the other person is doing can mean that you naturally start to mirror their posture. It can be difficult to do in a way that you feel comfortable about if you've not thought about it before so it is a good idea to practise with a willing friend first. Try different postures and mirror or try the opposite. What does it feel like?

Time to talk things through with a trusted colleague...

In building rapport with your team, thinking about your body language is as important as the words you use. In our training courses on coaching and leadership we often ask course members to try mirroring each other's behaviour and ask what it feels like, for example, if they are leaning back and the person talking to them has arms crossed and is on the edge of their chair – 'threatening!', and if they are sitting on the edge of the chair and the other person is sitting well back it feels 'as if they're not paying attention!'.

Lesson three: Working with consistency to enable change

We have already seen, in the example about the road safety, how important understanding consistency can be when we want people to do something new that they might not have felt was high on their agenda. The residents were more likely to agree to put a sign in their garden if they thought it was consistent with their position as people concerned about promoting careful driving.

Understanding consistency is equally important when we are thinking about supporting practitioners to change from something that they have held dear for a long time. The psychologists tell us that if we've done something a certain way for a long time, when someone comes along and asks us to do it differently, one of the reasons why we find this so hard is because subconsciously we are thinking: "If I do it her way, does that mean that I was a rubbish practitioner all those years doing it the other way?!". If you've ever struggled to persuade a practitioner to change to free-flow or introduce more spontaneous planning, that might be what is going on in the head of your practitioner. At some, largely subconscious level, she might be thinking:

> "If I agree to free-flow then does that mean that the first twenty years of my career I've been doing it all wrong? Am I a useless practitioner?".

A good example of this is found in the early years world of phonics. When I trained as a teacher over thirty years ago there had been a big reaction against a skills based approach to the teaching of reading. Children, we were told, needed to immerse themselves in books, understand context, read for meaning and pleasure. All this was certainly true. The evidence seemed to suggest that many children taught to read solely either through phonic decoding or word recognition reached a 'plateau' at around six from where their reading did not progress. It was thought at the time that this was connected to children's inability to 'read for meaning'. When Jim Rose published his report on phonics in 2005 many practitioners in the early years sector reacted strongly against it.

There were many reasons for this reaction and this book is not the place to go into them all, but one of the reasons is important for the work we are doing on motivation and change. I had welcomed the "real books" and "apprenticeship" approach and taught many children to read this way. If I accepted all the findings in Jim Rose's report would that mean that I had been a bad teacher for all those years? It was an uncomfortable feeling for a while, no less uncomfortable for being largely subconscious, and was only helped by the opportunity to talk and reflect with others on the different needs of children and changes in research base etc. I helped myself to see that:

a) It wasn't about phonics or reading for meaning – both were needed and still validated in the "simple view of reading" now being recommended

b) When I was first teaching there was real need to bring books and enjoying books into children's lives as they were missing in many places. We've done that, brought in the books and now we can afford to take more time thinking about how to develop children's phonological awareness

c) If I was honest I hadn't been that well taught at college about how to teach phonics and there was room for improvement, which I could learn from the new Letters and Sounds materials.

In other words I found a way to rationalise how my previous teaching was the right thing to do at that time, and how it can also be right to change my practice now. As leaders we will sometimes need to do this for ourselves, but also support practitioners through the process. Thinking back to the practitioner we began with reluctant to engage with free flow, you might want to first tap into the reasons why she did it

differently and then look for a way to rationalise how it was the right thing to do in the past, but this is a better option for now. For example, starting off with a bit of mirroring to acknowledge the real feelings...

"I can understand why the routine for the nursery used to have set times for outside play, and see why you're worried about health and safety. You had different age groups needing different kinds of provision in a very little space and no veranda at all. Also most of our children used to come from homes with gardens, but now the majority are living in flats and spending a lot of time in buggies with little chance to develop their physical skills. Now we've got a bigger space and a veranda I think we could plan something that would meet the needs of all children, keep them safe and give them more opportunities outdoors."

Enabling change

Low effect	1) Tidy up the spare clothes cupboard before asking parents for donations	2) Set up parents' notice board – display planning sheets
		3) Introduce a parents' suggestion box
		4) Reduce number of recorded observations – but make sure they are all really purposeful
		5) Start having agendas for staff meetings
		6) Spend more time listening to the children
		7) Contact NCB for more information on listening networks
		8) Invite parents in to read stories with the children in home languages
High effort	9) Move the shed from the front to the back of the nursery to provide more room for parents in the mornings	11) Introduce home visits
		12) Upgrade the toilets
	10) New curtains – old ones getting shabby	13) Trial new planning format
		14) Update the nursery brochure with our values and mission statement and how we want to involve parents
		15) Organise an evening event for parents to celebrate all the different cultures and start to engage them more in the life of the nursery
	Low impact	**High impact**

What	Why	Notes
Sensory room	To support children's learning and development across all five sense.	Not sure where it could go.
Update toilets	Old and shabby – difficult to keep clean.	
New curtains	Also old and shabby.	Faded but can cope with another wash until there is a bigger budget.
Update nursery brochure	To better reflect our vision and values and share our pedagogy with parents.	Wait until work with parents complete to reflect further on what we want to include. Also look for additional budget so we can do a professional job.
Move shed	More space for parents to gather in the mornings.	Not sure how to do this.

And then try the first small step:

> "What about if we try it on Wednesdays and Fridays when we've got more staff and see how it goes?".

Action planning

Action plans help you to draw together all the different things you need to move your setting from A to B. You may want to update your book area or work with your team on the characteristics of effective learning. You may have some external pressures to manage, perhaps recommendations from Ofsted or a request from the parents. Action plans help you to make sure that you have everything you need in place and a plan for putting them together over a particular period of time. What an action plan is not, is a piece of paper with boxes to fill in. Those pieces of paper can be useful – but only at the very end of the process.

The starting point is the self-evaluations and reflections you did in Chapter 3, combined with your vision for what you want the setting to become. From this will emerge a number of possible priorities for you and the team to work together on, in the ways I have presented.

Prioritising

The first thing to recognise is that you can't work on everything at the same time. You need to decide with your team; your owner, your headteacher, your governors or trustees, which of the possible areas for working on are going to be the most important for you this year, next year and beyond.

The best way to work through this is with lots of discussion and reflection time. The table on page 59 gives you an example of how one setting analysed their possibilities for action in order to help focus their priorities. The purpose of the grid (which was on a large piece of sugar paper) was to focus and record the discussion, not a replacement for talking.

The team used the grid after an away day when they'd done a lot of brainstorming to plot which of their ideas would have the most impact on children's progress and the quality of the provision and which would have the least. They also took into account how much effort each would take.

High effort includes things like lots of practitioner time, expense, resources, difficulty in persuading people to go along with the change etc. The idea is that if something is both high effort and low impact, you might not want to have it as such a high priority as something that can have a really big impact with minimum effort. The other thing to bear in mind is to check how many items you have in the 'high effort, high impact' box as there are only so many things you can do at once to be manageable.

The nursery decided that one of their priorities was about involving the parents more in the life of the nursery. They decided to work on the ideas highlighted in blue. They decided against moving the shed as although it would make for a nice area for parents to meet and talk it would take a lot of effort and expense to organise.

They also decided against updating the nursery brochure for the time being. They didn't feel that they had enough budget to do a really good job and also it might be something that they would do better when they'd spent more time working on parental involvement. The shed and the brochure therefore went on their "wish list".

Every setting should have a wish list. That's where you write down all the things you would like to do if you had infinite resources or energy. It's also where you include the things that you would like to do but for now just can't see being possible.

When they'd finished their prioritising discussions the nursery wish list looked like this (see page 60). The sensory room had been on the list for a while. That is how wish lists work. You keep them until something happens and you find you can do something you thought was impossible (it took my old school nearly 20 years to find the money to replace the ramshackle old windows, but they did it in the end – and I was invited to the celebration party along with all the governors who had been with the schools "wishing" for new windows at different times during those years!).

Sometimes you will take something off a list because you no longer want it. One setting I worked with put 'opening up a greengrocer's market stall' on their list because they were passionate about healthy eating and there were so few opportunities to buy cheap, good quality fruit and vegetables in the area. It was something they really wanted to do, but couldn't see how they would find the time or energy to tackle such a big project...until everything else was in place and they returned to their initial idea with enthusiasm.

As well as focusing on parents, the nursery decided to pull together some work on listening and to update their planning format to reflect this.

They also decided to introduce an agenda to their staff meetings and use this to help them check each week on progress with the things they were working on, including trying to be more focused in their use of observations.

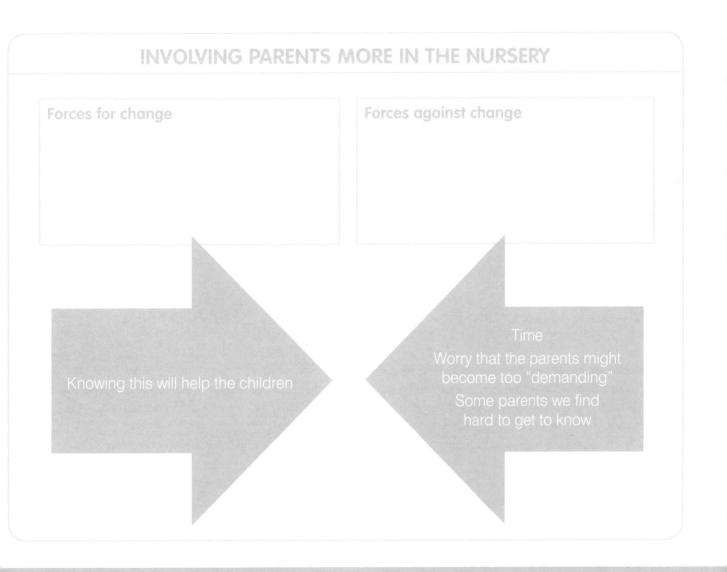

INVOLVING PARENTS MORE IN THE NURSERY

Forces for change

Forces against change

Knowing this will help the children

Time
Worry that the parents might become too "demanding"
Some parents we find hard to get to know

From prioritising to action

Having sorted out their priorities, the team is now working on how to put into practice their ambition to work more closely with parents. One useful technique for this stage in action planning is called **force field analysis**. This allows us to take a step back and think objectively about all the things that are going to help us with our task, and to identify (and hopefully put things in place to manage) those things that might get in the way, trip us up or provide the greatest challenge.

When the team looked at involving parents in this way, they were shocked to see that initially there seemed to be more things against the change than for it! (see page 61). It was important to get the hidden concerns out into the open so that they could be thought about and discussed. They not only identified more forces for change (e.g. the number of parents they already had good relationships with, the experience some members of staff had from other settings and potential time saved by having more effective relationships with all parents) – they also started to generate the ideas that became a practical action plan (see page 63).

Doing this kind of thinking before you write the 'plan' can help you think up strategies to move your plan on more smoothly. Once you've done all your thinking and talking it's useful to put down your ideas in an action plan so that you can focus on what you have to do, and when.

There are many different kinds of pro formas to help you with your action planning, but here is a simple example taken from the first part of the project exploring how to be more connected to their parents.

Involving all parents takes careful planning

The nursery in this project kept their action plans visible, on the notice board in the kitchen/staff room so that everybody kept in mind what they were doing and why.

KEY POINTS IN CHANGE AND ACTION PLANNING

In this chapter we started by looking at what is happening to us and our team when we experience change, drawing some lessons from the world of psychology to help us help others through change more effectively. We then looked at the process of making change happen: action planning.

- How do you support your staff so that they feel good about what they are doing now, but also good about working towards an even better future?

How do you feel about change yourself? How can this help you gain insights to enable you to support your staff positively through even difficult transitions?

Who writes your action plans? When? And How?

Where are they kept and how do you monitor the progress you make?

Practical action planning

What do we want to achieve? (outcomes and context)	Involve more parents in the life of the nursery			
Actions	**Who**	**When?**	**Notes**	✓
1 Check numbers – who is involved now and what they are doing.	Luz and Fran	7th Feb	Think about how we gather and keep this sort of information for the future.	
2 Walk round the rooms to check how inclusive they are for parents – different languages, pictures etc.	Maya and Chair	17th Feb		
3 Organise new displays, resources etc. to make sure pre-school reflects local community. Invite parents in to share languages with the staff and the children.	Maya and the team	25th March	Luz to have worked out a budget with the committee by 24th February. Plan to be in place by 25th March and orders completed – but making things happen in the classes will be implemented over the Summer term.	
4 Make sure that at least one member of staff is outside to meet and greet parents every morning.	Luz	From 7th Feb	Organise rota – make sure that there is cover as a priority even on difficult days.	
5 Put up noticeboard for parents in entrance.	Mercy	15th Feb	Ask some of the parents we know well for ideas about what to put up initially.	
6 Organise a feedback box or notice area to get parents' comments.	Mercy	15th Feb	Talk to parents about what sort of thing might work best to get useful feedback. Think how to manage expectations so that parents don't get disappointed if we can't do everything they suggest (this identified on force-field analysis as a possible issue).	
7 Staff meeting to plan events, new ways of organising parents evenings, starting routines etc. based on information learned in first part of the project.	Fran	24th March		

Conclusion

What happens next?

We are now, of course, using the revised EYFS 2012, looking for (and mostly finding) interesting opportunities amongst the challenges to make sure that we keep ourselves and our teams energised and motivated. We have found out more about the extension of the free entitlement for two-year-olds and received the new guidance for EYFSPs.

Looking into the future, the one thing that we can be certain of is that change will continue, and that we will experience low points and high ones as our own learning journey progresses. As leaders, we will need to continue to be able to respond to the priorities of the moment, whilst finding a way to remain true to the principles of early childhood that drew us into the profession in the first place. We will need to continue to motivate our teams and provide them with support and challenge, whilst looking after our own vision and sense of purpose.

In order to continue to be effective we will need to keep in touch with our strengths, so that we can draw on them flexibly when required.

A useful habit for times when you are feeling less confident or experiencing particularly challenging situations, can be to take time at the end of a day, a week or a month to think about what strengths you have shown and the difference that has made. Are you a particularly good listener? Do you have a talent for inspiring people with new ideas? Are you conscientious and get things done? Have you worked hard to learn how to give constructive feedback? Can you make people smile on dark days? Do parents trust and confide in you?

Also remember that you are not alone, however often it might feel like that. We have a strong, articulate and passionate early years community and we can draw support from each other through our personal and professional networks. If you don't know the answer to a question, or can't see your way around a particularly perplexing problem, phone a friend!

Whilst so much has changed, it is important to also remember that some things do stay the same. For example, our belief in the value of early childhood being important in its own right (as well as providing a strong foundation for a fulfilled future life), goes back to pioneers such as Froebel and Margaret McMillian.

Change can also be inspiring: looking more closely at the new things in early years, so many of them are hugely stimulating and exciting. How wonderful it is that we know more about brain development in young children. How exciting that we can now draw on research from other countries to learn more, for example Reggio Emilia in Italy and Te Whakaari in New Zealand.

We've also learned more about how to motivate and lead people. The research is telling us that we don't have to be authoritative, commanding army-style managers, that there is a place for the early years values of respect, listening and being positive when we work with adults as well as with children.

Being a leader in the early years sector may not be the easiest of roles, but it continues to be one of the most rewarding and intriguing. There is always something new to learn, to do, to think about – and we know what we do really matters.

Books and websites

- Brady, C. and Brady, T. (2000) *Rules of the Game*, Pearson Education.

I Bridges, W. (1991) *Managing Transitions Reading*, MA: Addison-Wesley.

I Davys and Bedow (2010) *Best Practice in Professional Supervision*, Jessica Kingsley Publishers.

I EYFS (2012) (http://www.foundationyears.org.uk/quality-provision/early-years-foundation-stage-framework/).

I Fullan, M. (2003) *The Moral Imperative of School Leadership*, Corwin Press.

I Fullan, M. (2011) *The Moral Imperative Realised*, Corwin Press.

I Garvey, D. and Lancaster, A. (2010) *Leadership for Quality in Early Years and Playwork*, NCB.

I Goldstein, M. and Cialdini (2007), *Yes! 50 Secrets from the science of Persuasion*, Profile Books, London.

I Goleman, D., Boyatzis, R. and McKee, A. (2002) *The New Leaders*, Sphere, London.

I Moyles, J. (2006) *Effective Leadership and Management in the Early Years*, OUP.

I Pask, R. and Joy, B. (2011) *Mentoring Coaching*, Open University Press.

I Pre-school Learning Alliance (2010) *Developing Effective Teamwork* (www.pre-school.org.uk).

I Rodd, J. (2006), *Leadership in Early Childhood*, OUP.

I Rogers, J (2007) *Adults Learning*, OUP.

I Rogers, J. (2009), *Coaching Skills*, OUP.

- Siraj-Blatchford, I. & Manni, L. (2007) *Effective Leadership in the Early Years Sector* (www.ioe.ac.uk/publications).

I Smith, A. and Langston, A. (1999) *Managing Staff in Early Years Settings*, Routledge.

I Sylva, K., Sammons, P., Mehuish, E., Siraj-Blatchford, I., Taggart, B., Hunt, S. and Jelicic, H. (2008), *Effective Pre-School and Primary Education 3-11 Project (EPPE 3-11)* (www.ioe.ac.uk/publications).

- Whelan, Fenton, (2009) *Lessons Learned*, MPG Books Group.

- Whitmore, J. (2002) *Coaching for Performance*, Nicholas Brearly, London.

I Visit http://www.businessballs.com/ for practical summaries and information on many leadership tools and techniques, for example the Johari Window, Belbin, Maslow.

Acknowledgements

This book was inspired by the work on leadership that I have been doing with colleagues at Robert Owen Early Years Centre in Greenwich. It has been a delight to work in such an inspirational and welcoming environment and I would like to thank everybody from Robert Owen and Greenwich who made it all possible, including the children who feature in the lovely photographs. I would also like to thank all the leaders and aspiring leaders from schools, nurseries and pre-schools who have been part of the training and coaching this year, and who have contributed so much to my thinking about what it means to be a leader in the early years in the 21st Century. Your energy and resourcefulness never fails to impress.

A big thank you also goes to my colleagues at Linden Learning for their patience and support in getting the book finished to the deadline and in decent order.

Thank you to the staff and parents who gave their permission to use the photos in this book.

Finally, whilst all case studies and examples are drawn from thirty years of experience in the sector, the individual details and contexts have all been changed. Any similarity to real people and events is therefore totally coincidental.

.... And the learning journey continues: for all of us